The Frustrated women's club

something to be disregarded. We want to be our own person, but we are also still afraid of the *chhittar*[1] that this might warrant from our parents. We want to live by our own values, no matter how different those are from the values we grew up with, and yet not be regarded as a disrespectful prick by our family. It's not a lot to ask for, but sometimes, as an IM, it is.

Hello. I am Alia. Alia Arora. And I am an IM, but a particularly messy one because I'm also a Middle East baby. I grew up in Abu Dhabi, about an hour's drive in good traffic from Dubai, where I now live. It's not too far away from India, but far enough that I can be described as being "disconnected from (my) roots" every time I do or suggest something not typically Indian. I have never lived in India and I have no desire to live in India, so if my parents say that I am disconnected from my roots, they're probably right. If I could find a way to do it, I would be my own nationality.

I believe there are two kinds of roots anyway. There are ethnic roots, the roots that bind you to your culture. I feel quite connected to my Punjabi ethnic roots. I love the music, the dance, the food, the culture, the language, the history, the alcoholism (what? who said that?), the everything. It's something I grew up with and there's much to enjoy there.

Then there are the roots that connect you to your nationality. In my case, that's India. I find that so strange, though. I did not grow up in India and cannot imagine ever having to live in India, but I am Indian. It is a part of my identity that

1   Punjabi word for 'slap'

11

I don't identify with at all. If I wanted to (and had immigration laws' approval) I could fly away to Canada or Australia or America or any number of places where one might find people like me, and shed my current nationality. My ethnicity is not something I can change; my nationality is.

So, here I am, a Punjabi Middle East baby with ties to the Western world through education and a consequently confused state of mind about who I really am. Welcome to my blog, where I will share with you the contemporary dilemmas that accompany the Indian Millennial's life. I have done the impossible. As a single Indian girl in my twenties, I have accomplished the highly coveted task of moving out of my parents' house and into the greatest city on earth, Dubai. For any non-Indians reading this, this might not seem particularly remarkable, being something that most people in their twenties would be expected to do. But Indian culture doesn't work that way. The wish to move out of the parental home is a direct insult to the parents. 'Do we not give you a comfortable home to live in? Are we having problems?' they ask. So when I put forth the prospect of potentially moving out of my parents' house, they were immediately offended. 'Do we not allow you to live your life freely? Is our relationship a struggle for you? Maybe letting you go to the West for your education was a bad idea. You don't respect Indian culture at all now.'

'It has nothing to do with our relationship or our culture,' I said. 'I just need my own space. And imagine having to drive all the way to Dubai from Abu Dhabi every single day. My day will be completely taken up by work and the commute. I won't have a life left outside of work.'

It took a lot of convincing, but my parents finally made their peace with me wanting to move out. I think that's worth recording, because I could be making history.

Finding Sassy Alia

In my pursuit to turn over a new leaf, I made up my mind to not be the twenty-four-year-old child I left behind in Abu Dhabi and instead become the twenty-four-year-old woman I wanted to be.

In my posh new Downtown Dubai flat, I was not going to be University Alia. University Alia was the person who would try on fifteen different outfits and leave them lying crumpled on her bed. She would then come back home and move the pile of clothes from the bed to the chair, where they would stay for the next few weeks.

I wanted to change that. Downtown Alia couldn't be a high-powered career-driven woman and still be the woman who waited until her absolute last set of knickers was worn out before doing her laundry. I was going to be organised; everything was going to be put away into their designated spots. I was going to become a (non-terrifying) combination of Marie Kondo and my mother, and declutter my life.

My mother has always been far too involved in my life—and my clutter—than I think healthy and polite.

'Alia, your clothes literally fall out of your cupboard when I open the door.'

'Well, why are you in my room, Mother?' I say, stifling the urge to gently push her toward the door.

She glares at me. 'What are you trying to hide?'

'Nothing', I say, thinking about the vibrator in my sock drawer that a drunken evening in Amsterdam pushed me to buy. Could I convince her it's a massage device? What if she wants to use it, though? What if she tries to use it for a foot massage? I wouldn't be able to view the vibrator the same way again.

But those days are now behind me. My vibrator can live on my bedside table. It's the beginning of a new chapter in my life. A new job in the bustling Dubai International Financial Centre. A new home in Downtown Dubai, without my parents. The same old set of friends that I managed to persuade to move to Dubai after we finished university in London. I am going to be the woman they show in films, except that instead of London or New York, I'll be in Dubai... which is far better anyway.

I'll be the kind of woman who wakes up in the morning with glowing skin and perfect hair and who doesn't struggle to find the iron because she got her clothes neatly pressed and ready the night before. She prepares a healthy breakfast smoothie and doesn't have a craving for a turkey and cheese croissant. She consumes the breakfast smoothie on her commute, and once she is at her desk, her switch is turned on and she is ready to tackle the day. When she is done tackling the day, she tackles male dominance by lifting the most amount of weight in the free weights section at the gym. She walks out of the gym with pride and stops at Spinneys to fill up her shopping trolley with organic vegetables, lean meats, fruits, and perhaps a sensible 90 percent dark chocolate. On the weekend, she paints the town red with her friends but does it in a classy way so that no questionable stories end up on Instagram.

At present, however, I am not that kind of woman.

I am the kind of woman who doesn't know how to hammer a nail into the wall, so I call the maintenance team in the building. When they see that I am but a young girl, they help me get the logistics of my life together. Not only do they hammer all the nails into the wall, they plug in the TV, connect the printer, and get the phone line running. I want to tell them that I am a strong, independent woman who doesn't need a man to fix these things for her, but I also want to give them a big ol' hug for saving me hours on YouTube, watching "how to get the phone line running".

Last year, fresh out of uni, I had booked my final London–Abu Dhabi flight. I had said goodbye to so many things. I had said goodbye to Dave, my boyfriend of two weeks. Well, I say boyfriend, but I only use it as a term to dignify what we had. What we had was a series of shagalicious episodes followed by some excessively racy photos I sent him that I now wish I could get back. But at least that taught me a lesson. Never leave a trace on someone else's phone.

My London friends didn't really understand the Gulf. They thought that because I was from Abu Dhabi, I was a proper G. The assumption that everyone made was that I was a rich child who lived in a mansion with gold chandeliers, ate off silver plates, and snacked on caviar. Some of them would ask me if the dumbbells in my local gym in Abu Dhabi were made of gold, and if my mode of transportation to and from school had been a camel. Others would ask even dumber questions. 'Is Dubai the capital of Saudi?' 'Dubai is the capital of nothing', I would answer.

I said goodbye to all those friends. All the memories. I said goodbye to the Alia I had become, the Alia I had transformed into from the shy, timid Schoolgirl Alia I had been back in Abu Dhabi.

Sassy London Alia was confident about herself. Abu Dhabi Alia, on the other hand, was overshadowed by her parents and their decisions and wishes. Sassy Alia had about 3,400 miles of distance from her parents, so I could see why she was sassy and did shit without the risk of being caught, or worse, disowned.

Now, however, it feels like there is another chance to be Sassy Alia. The distance between me and my parents has increased, for sure. It's not 3,400 miles, but at this stage I can work with any distance that is more than that between their bedroom and my bedroom. This could be my chance to explore expat life in the UAE free of the voices of my parents in my head.

There won't be the voice of my mother saying, 'Alia, try and come home on time. Your father and I have to be up early tomorrow.'

When I countered this with, 'Why do I have to come home early if *you* want to wake up early tomorrow?' I received a very Indian telling off.

'If you don't come home, we'll be worried sick about you. We won't be able to sleep.'

'Why are you worried? I'm just out with some friends. I don't have to take public transport, either. I'll be in my own car.'

'What if you get kidnapped on the empty highway on your way home?'

'If it's an empty highway, how is someone going to kidnap me? I'll just drive by them.'

'What if your car breaks down? What if there's an accident?'

'I'll call 999 and stay inside the car until they come.'

'Just come home early. I am not in the mood for these illogical arguments with you.'

What pissed me off about that particular encounter was the fact that I was not the one being illogical and yet I was made to sound like the illogical one. What pissed me off even more was that the exchange between us was starting to sound increasingly like that between a teenager and her mother. The fifteen-year-old across the street and I were having the same arguments with our mothers, and it was embarrassing for only one of us.

But now, things can be different. I can officially start living the life that expats who don't live with their parents do. How exciting is this?

Abu Dhabi is Just a Car Ride Away

I was wrong. My parents are not as technologically challenged as I would like them to be and so have taken to keeping track of my activities through Instagram stories. When I posted a story from a club called Inka at four o'clock in the morning, my mother saw it and *shudder* replied.

Mum: Are you at a club?? Right now??
Alia: Mum, why are you up at 4?
Mum: Some of us like to wake up early and pray to the Lord
Alia: Are you being catty with me?
Mum: No, I'm just asking if you're at a club right now.
Alia: I am.
Mum: Okay, enjoy.

Was she being sarcastic? I can't tell with my parents sometimes. I feel like there is a very thin line between their backhanded comments/taunts and actual concern. Thin as human hair.

Still, life in Dubai has been rewarding so far.

I have just started working for a business publication called *The EMEA Bank*. My job is to dig around and put together articles that will help potential investors understand the market risks better and make informed decisions about whether or not they should be bringing their capital into the market. That's the theory, anyway. I'm still figuring out what it all means, but the job is actually way more interesting than it sounds, and I'm thoroughly enjoying the looks I get from shopkeepers and passers-by at DIFC when I walk around. I catch my reflection and give myself a small smile. I have on high heels, and even though they do make life a little more challenging than it needs to be, I like that they add a bit of an air to my person, like I am a high-powered, driven, career girl who doesn't get affected by uncomfortable high heels. After several attempts on my first morning to put my long, jet-black hair up in a ponytail failed, I now settle for a messy bun, which is also proving to be the right choice, because high-powered, driven, career girls don't have time for complicated hairstyles.

Still, a new job is nothing short of terrifying. It's like being in a video game with no idea of the rules. Like a Grand Theft Auto Office version, but instead of ammunition, you get a computer and you don't kill any prostitutes. Your character is dressed in formal wear, standing clueless in a big office. The only cheat code you have is the fact that everyone is an expat.

The Dubai equivalent of talking about the weather in London is the question 'Where are you from?' No one gets offended if you ask them this question and it will easily take up the next ten minutes of conversation, because for an expat in the UAE, there is always a story about how they ended up here.

'I'm from Boston, but my boyfriend got a job in Dubai so I came after him. Now we're engaged!' Of all my new colleagues,

Aisling is probably the closest to becoming an actual friend. She's in the Research department, same as me.

'I'm from Essex and my husband, Mark, is from Wales', said Laura. 'We were both in the London office and when they started expanding into Dubai, they needed someone to come down here to set it up', she added with a smile. 'We haven't been able to move back somehow!' Laura immediately gave me goals for what I wanted to be: an elegant woman exuding badass vibes.

'I grew up here but my family come from Kerala in India', said Joy.

Ah, the conversation with Joy. *You and I are alike, aren't we? We like to say we're from here, but for anyone looking at documents, we'd be from India. Do we want to go to India, though? Absolutely fucking not (pardon my French).*

They ask 'Where is home?' and we look at them like they're crazy. 'Here?' we say slowly, confused as to what other answer they were expecting. Of course, home is here. Not on paper, but in our heads, yes. The longest I have ever spent in India is three weeks, and that's not long at all, is it? Most of the time was spent in the homes of our distant family, witnessing Indian hospitality at its best.

Visiting one's Indian family "back home" is basically about having a feast. The host will serve a multitude of starters and insist that you try each of them and multiple servings of each of them because if you don't, they'll insist that they'll be cross with you. You eat up, trying to make them happy. They then lay out the main course. 'There's more?!' is the question uppermost in all the guests' minds. You wonder how your stomach could possibly hold all that but you eat up again anyway, because you don't want anyone to be cross. Finally, a selection of dessert comes out and you feel like you can see the light at the end of the tunnel. One more serving to go, you think. And then the hostess says, 'Tea?' and you can't possibly say no to tea.

Having spent most of our time in people's homes, expanding our stomach capacity to accommodate all that food, I never got to know the country that I apparently belong to. The tiny amount of time we had left, we spent in street markets looking for cheap Indian delights to take as souvenirs for the other kids in school.

So, yes, when people like me and Joy are asked where we are from and where home is, the answer is decidedly 'here'.

I spent my first week getting to know people and fully abusing my friends' knowledge of Dubai haunts. If a place has been deemed Instagrammable, I will be there. If it's "the place to be" on a "Top 10 Restaurants to Try Out if You're a Fan of the Mediterranean Diet" list, I will be there. If it's trending, I will be there. I am not always a basic bitch, but I can experiment with it.

But as my parents never fail to remind me, Abu Dhabi is only a short drive from home and so, on the weekends, it apparently makes no sense to stay in Dubai. I could beg to differ, but I would also be begging for another lecture on the importance of sticking together as a family.

Mum: Come for dinner. (This text is to the family group.)

Trisha is typing...
I stare at the screen.

Trisha: What's the plan? What time should we come?

Mum: You and Balveer can come whenever you like. Alia, try to be here at 6. You'll need to leave early if you're going back to Dubai after.

Is this is a ploy to make me stay the night? If I stay the night, will they then try and convince me to move back home? Probably not.

Alia: I'll stay the night.

The drive to Abu Dhabi is one of the best things to happen to the world of transport. Imagine a long stretch of highway, an uninterrupted playlist on the phone with cheesy music from the eighties, nineties, and noughties, and a full tank of petrol.

At home I'm greeted by the familiar smell of Mum's cooking and the sound of the telly playing old Bollywood tunes. I look out the French window into the backyard and make out the figure of my father swinging a golf club. I can imagine he'd rather be at the golf course instead of at dinner, but I can also imagine the look of horror on my mother's face if he ever suggested missing dinner to play golf. It makes sense that he has gone with the option of staying in tonight.

As we settle in, chatter about life in Dubai takes over the conversation.

Mum asks me about my daily routine. This is her way of asking whether or not I get up to any unholy shenanigans. I do, but I must hide this.

'I get to work around nine o'clock', I say. 'Stay until about six. Go to the gym. Get dinner. Then maybe drinks with some friends', I add, looking up to see their reaction. I don't want to lie to them, but I also don't want to get into trouble. Understanding their reaction will help me understand what more I can let them know about.

Is Mum going to bring up the story on Instagram from Inka at four o'clock in the morning? Will it lead to another one of those lectures about safety that I know off by heart? I just want dinner; can we skip this? Because, Mum, you and I both know that no matter what you say, I will still do what I like. Also, I'm not an idiot. If it isn't safe, I won't do it. I am not particularly interested in dying.

'Mm-hmm.' Mum nods. 'And any boyfriends?'

Oh. We've gone in a completely different direction.

'Um', I start. 'No.'

Mum and Dad look at each other. Dad seems a bit more uncomfortable than Mum. I can imagine. Being a dad and thinking about your daughter's potential boyfriend must be taxing. Your little girl being defiled by a man you don't even know? Lord.

'I have a friend', Dad starts. 'At the country club.'

My eyebrows immediately start to rise.

'He has a friend, who has a son about your age.'

Friends—specifically, Indian female friends—can you guess what's about to happen?

Your father has a friend who has a friend who has a son about your age. One out of these two possible scenarios can happen. Which will it be?

1. Nothing, because they each lead independent lives without each other's knowledge and the idea of ever dating each other does not cross your mind because it's icky, not hot.

OR

2. 'Alia, there's a *rishta*[2] for you.'

I can tell you just how desi[3] you are by your answer.

If you picked 1 and are Indian: I am jealous of your upbringing.

If you oscillated between 1 and 2: Do you understand how life works?

If you picked 2 with conviction: Welcome to the desi club.

If you picked 2 and further imagined two middle-age Indian men giving each other an awkward dad hug saying '*ab waqt aa gaya hai hum is dosti ko rishtedaari mein badaldein*' (translation: 'it's time we turned this friendship into a relationship'): Welcome to the Frustrated Women's Club.

I look at my dad. Is this his idea of a joke? He likes to make jokes, Dad does. He's just taking this one a bit too far.

'You're joking', I finally chuckle with a sigh. 'This is a joke, right?'

Mum looks at me with a frown. 'It's not funny', she says. 'You're twenty-four now.'

'Yes, I'm *only* twenty-four.'

'Twenty-four isn't young.'

'Of course it's young, Mum! Just yesterday I was watching a *Mr. Bean* episode on YouTube. I'm a child.'

'That's ridiculous. We started looking for boys for Trisha when she was twenty-two.'

'Just because you were doing it, doesn't mean it was the right thing to do.'

---

2 potential suitor for marriage
3 of or belonging to the Indian subcontinent

As things start to heat up between me and Mum, Dad tries to take over.

'Alia', he says calmly. 'We are not asking you to marry him right away. Just have a look at what he's like, and if you like him, you could think about getting married.'

Marriage. Marriage. Marriage.

No matter how many times I say it in my head, the word still sounds strange, especially if I am going to be involved. I am no stranger to the marriage phenomenon, of course. One look at my Instagram page will tell you that it's marriage season all year round.

I am not against the concept of marriage. A legal commitment that binds two individuals together—there's nothing dodgy about that at all. But me, getting married? I can't do that. I've been single for far too long. The only time in my life I wasn't single was the two weeks I was with Dave, and if we're being strictly technical, that didn't count. That wasn't a relationship. That was a thing furthest from a relationship.

It was a period of unholy shenanigans. *Haram.* Sex with a white man has to be the most haram thing I could have done as an Indian girl. Haram that, frankly, wasn't actually worth it. The entire two weeks was like running toward the finish line and always falling to the ground seconds before I could get there. And I'm certain that Dave was hunting for more singles in the area while we were still together. No part of our two-week association spelt "relationship". And if I'm being honest, the idea of a relationship makes me shit bricks. Can you imagine what marriage would do? It's too much of an ask. Marry someone out of the blue? What a notion!

'Is this why you asked me to come early?' I finally say after a few seconds.

Mum turns to look at Dad. 'Yes', she says.

'Okay, honestly, I'm not ready for this. At all. I haven't even been in a relationship. How am I going to just marry someone out of the blue?'

'We are not asking you to marry him', Dad chimes in. 'Just meet him. See if there's... attraction.'

'Ew', I say. 'Ew. Dad, never talk to me about attraction again.'

Dads should not be allowed to talk about attraction to their daughters. I can't be the only one to react this way. This is just like the time my father had "the talk" with me before I went away to university. He took me out for a walk one evening before I was due to fly out and started the conversation with the most awkward opening sentence in the history of verbal conversation.

'Alia, you're eighteen years old and I'm sure you'll have... urges.'

I turned to look at him with a look that can only be described as mortified. 'Are you about to tell me where babies come from? Because I know, so you can spare us this conversation.'

Dad scowled. 'I'm just saying that you're going to live on your own for the first time. You might have urges. Don't act on those urges. You can drink but no drugs. If you do act on those urges and you get pregnant, you tell me. I won't be mad.'

That was one awkward conversation. And this, what was happening right now, was an even more awkward conversation.

'All I'm saying is, there's nothing wrong in meeting someone', Dad concludes.

Newton's First Law states that a body in motion at constant velocity will continue to stay in motion unless acted upon by an external force. I feel like a body in constant motion at a constant velocity and feel an immense level of empathy for this object that Newton theorised. What are these external, unbalanced forces acting upon this object in steady motion? Is the object asking for it? Is the object happy in the state of motion? Can you not find it within you to treat this object with respect and let it be? Why are you disturbing the course of nature? Step away from the object. Let the object be, you nincompoop.

So, What Do You Think of the Guy?

'Has Mum told you her plan for you?' Trisha says when she sees me sitting glumly on the sofa.

Trisha and Balveer have just arrived and the party is now in full swing. She hands over a bottle of malbec to me as I nod. 'Thought you might need this', she says with a sympathetic smile. I don't know if she's enjoying my torture or if she will be my genuine support system tonight and all future nights when my father, of all people, chooses to meddle with my love life.

Balveer joins us. Trisha's husband of two years. Her constant companion through good times and bad. Constantly available to tease me. Now smiling at me with raised eyebrows as if to say, 'I'm finding this all hilarious, little sister.'

'Stop smiling', I say, punching his arm playfully.

'Alia is going to be Mrs. Dull and Boring Alia', he adds with a grin, knowing my worst nightmare only too well. His smile quickly fades, though, when Trisha and my mother turn to look at him.

'We're married. We aren't dull and boring', Trisha says.

'Of course we aren't.' Balveer nods and then winks at me.

I shake my head. So this is what life will be.

I will be a married woman one day. Yuck.

A married woman. I will have a *roka*[4] ceremony. I will post a photo on Instagram announcing this engagement. Cousins from India will say 'you've been roka-fied' and I will cringe. Why do they call it roka-fied anyway? Surely, roka-ed makes more sense?

Family from the US, Canada, the UK, India, and family friends from Dubai and Abu Dhabi will all congratulate me and my Man. They'll start making old jokes about marriage. Jokes about how the man is so repressed in the marriage, which is hilarious when you think about the institutionalised patriarchy we live in. The absolute worst jokes are the ones that end up as chain messages on my father's phone. One of them had a "Before Marriage" caption under a photo of a couple looking rather happy as the man lifts her in his arms. The next photo was the same couple except the caption read "After Marriage" and the woman seemed to have gained a lot of weight and was now lifting her husband in her arms. How hilarious that the woman gained so much weight after her wedding!

We'll go wedding clothes shopping. When Trisha got married, we hit stores in the infamous Chandni Chowk in New Delhi, India. It was the single most traumatic experience of my life. The lanes reminded me of a cramped library, except it wasn't a library. It was the complete opposite of a library. It

4   ceremony to make a couple official. Literally translates to 'stopped', indicating that the search for a partner is over or has been 'stopped'

was the thing furthest from a Quiet Zone. It was the loudest and smelliest place I had ever been in.

But apparently the outfits and wedding trinkets in Chandni Chowk were second to none, and so for my sister, for her wedding, for her happiness, I had to martyr myself. In the end, Dad and I spent the entire time sitting in the corners of the shops, looking like dejected boyfriends while our girlfriends shopped.

Now, I will be expected to martyr myself for my own wedding. Even the notion. I am not going back to Chandni Chowk.

We will have a wedding. Photographers will make us do silly poses for the camera. One at the henna ceremony, where I will have to hold up my hands in front of the camera and smile shyly, showing off the henna design. One at the engagement party, of me and Man exchanging rings and showing off our ring fingers in front of the camera. Another one at the wedding, me showing off my *choora*[5].

Once the wedding is over, we'll be expected to attend dinner parties in honour of the happy couple. We'll be made to sit through societal small talk. We will have to laugh at every sexist joke that every Uncle makes at every party. You know these jokes will happen, and there's nothing you can do about them.

What if we live with Man's parents? When his mother has to go to a party, she might ask me to accompany her. That's not even the worst part. What if she takes me with her to IKEA? What then? What if we live in the suburbs? What if they expect me to push two Punjabi kids out of my clackers? My clackers

5   bangles that a newlywed woman wears

are my business, but that doesn't stop people requesting for it to release multiple kids. No matter how much I don't want them.

I can't have this happen to me. No. Not now. Possibly a long-term relationship. A wedding could be far out on the horizon. Kids? Fuck no. My clackers are my clackers.

Mum is frantically passing every dish to Balveer, because as the son-in-law of the family, he can't possibly be overlooked. Trisha is scowling at the extra attention he commands simply by virtue of being a man.

'So, what do you think of the guy then?' Trisha says to me.

'She hasn't seen him yet', Dad says. 'I'll ask Mr. Sawhney from the club to send a picture across.'

'What's his name?' I say from across the table.

'Samar Grewal.'

I resolutely change the conversation after this, and the rest of the evening goes by well enough with the usual pleasant bantering and bickering. After dinner, I bid goodnight to Trisha, Balveer, and my parents and curl up in the duvet in my childhood bedroom, hoping for the bed to absorb me, for it to end me right here, in my prime.

I retrieve my phone from inside my pocket and open Facebook.

Samar Grewal

There are four or five results, but one stands out as the most relevant.

Samar Grewal
Lives in Dubai
From Dubai
Auditor at PwC

There is a drowning sensation in my stomach. This has to be the one.

I click his profile.

Another drowning sensation.

Well, fuckity fuck.

I stare at his profile picture for a few seconds. He looks like a very typical man from the Sikh Punjabi community. He has on a white cap, covering his hair that presumably has been tied into a bun, as all Sikh men do. He has a beard and moustache and a toothy smile. No, that's not it. Yes, his teeth are visible. But his gums too. What do you call that? It can't be a gummy smile, can it? Whatever it is, it isn't doing it for me.

Maybe there are better pictures of him? a small voice says in my head. Who is that? Is that Reasonable Alia? Go away, Reasonable Alia. If a man has a better picture, trust me, he's using it. What you see is what you get. What I see is not attractive, so what makes you think that what I get will be?

Reasonable Alia shrugs and walks away. Her tenure is short-lived. Still, I swipe through his pictures. Plenty of pictures in clubs and pubs, some from holidays in America, and some from villages in Punjab. His photos make him seem quite normal. Too normal. Bordering on ordinary. Is this where my glorious single life comes to an end?

No, fuck no, Alia. Sassy Alia? Is that you? *The one and only. And I'm here to tell you this is not the one for you.* How can you be so sure? *Well, so many of us feel so icky about him?* Icky? *He wears a cap to cover his long hair, Alia. It's icky.* Ugh, of course you're right. Should never have doubted the wisdom of so many Alias.

I take screenshots of the pictures and send them through to Trisha and Balveer individually.

Trisha: Did Dad send these to you?

Alia: No, I stalked him on Facebook. Do not share these with them. I need to know what you think first.

Trisha: Hmm. I mean, he isn't extraordinarily handsome but he isn't the worst. You should give it a go.

I raise an eyebrow. That isn't what I was looking for. Moments later, a text comes through from Balveer.

Balveer: Wow. Young Jatt from the Pind.
Alia: What do you think?
Balveer: He looks like a Jatt from the Pind.
Alia: Is that a good thing or a bad thing?
Balveer: Am I on the record?
Alia: Do you want to be?
Balveer: No.
Alia: Okay, off the record, what do you think?
Balveer: Off the record, you can do better.

I smile. That's what I want to hear. Might need to use Balveer as my upper hand when the moment of truth comes. 'Mum, Dad, it's a hard pass for me. Even Balveer agrees.' Balveer will be pissed off because he did go off the record, but surely he can take one for the team.

Many Drinks Are Needed

You know how some weekends leave you more exhausted than the week preceding them? Last weekend was one of those. I spent Saturday night at home in Abu Dhabi and then faked a work emergency that required my urgent attention to get out early on Sunday morning, all the while messaging the group text chain that houses my two closest friends, Sanjay and Meher.

S.A.M.

Alia: If you're in the mood for hot goss, shall we gathereth later this evening?

Sanj: Why do you sound like a nobleman?

Alia: Because I was fucked this weekend. Not in a good way. It's messed up my wires big time.

Sanj: Lol what?

Alia: Will you come out for drinks or not?

Meher: Oh no, what happened? You alright?

Alia: Got fucked. Deets later. Meet at 7? Downtown?

Sanj: Done-zo.

Meher: See you then.

Sanjay, Meher, and I have been friends since school. While Sanjay and I had a reputation of being troublemakers, Meher was the sensible one. Well, I say troublemakers, but in reality, we met at something called The Bright Students' Club that was organised by the teachers to bring together students expected to get the highest grades. The idea was to give us additional schoolwork to stretch us, but all we did was gossip on the phone every night. I would tell Sanjay about the guys I thought were good looking and he would tell me details as to why they would be no good for me. I would then return the favour except I would find him decent girls instead of just proclaiming that they'd be no good. Much more useful.

As school faded into the past, we grew into adults with proper degrees and jobs. Meher became a graphic designer as she always wanted to be, and Sanjay became a lawyer, which I will forever find pretty hilarious. For someone who I always expected to end up on the wrong side of the law, Sanjay has done well for himself. Life did change but we still bank on each other for the support, the reality checks, the laughter, and the friendship. I think the strongest bonding moment for me and Sanjay was when I got sick at a club in London and he held back my hair for me and didn't get sick himself but instead gave me a glass of water and did not judge me one bit. He's a real pal.

For me and Meher, the bond strengthened through countless nights of girly gossip. We chatted about boys—of course we did—and spent more time than strictly necessary to Facebook-stalk said boys. Boys would "poke" us on Facebook and we would poke them back (not a euphemism) and start conversations with them, tease them, and never chat to them again because why not.

But Meher always had one foot in the real world and deep down is truly sensible. I don't think she ever had any arguments with her parents about wanting to stay out late at night, or ever yell 'It's *my* life!' I have always known her to solve disagreements calmly instead of with a raised voice, something I want to accomplish myself.

I rely on Sanjay to mess up with me and give me terrible advice from the male perspective, and we both rely on Meher to help us fix our shit. It's the perfect balance. This is why three-person groups are the best. There's always going to be at least one sane person in any given situation, one person who isn't drinking and hence can take up the open position of designated driver, and be the person whose life provides goals for the other two.

I have spent all day fixating on my one goal: how to get rid of this new inconvenience. I refuse to brand him as anything else. He is not a potential partner. I am not looking for a partner. We will not date. A date is something that two people who fancy each other go out on. From his photo, I already know there is no fancying going on for me.

There are some voices in my head saying things like *Alia, no, you should give this man a chance, you haven't even met him*, but I'm shutting those voices out because they don't belong to me. They belong to my mother. There is also another prominent voice in my head just saying *what the fuck* constantly. That voice seems more authentic, so I am taking it upon myself as a primary task to listen to that voice rather than my mother's.

Come six o'clock, I change into a top and a leather miniskirt that I bought after moving out to celebrate that my mum was no longer able to comment on my clothes, and head down to the Downtown bar we've been frequenting since we were legally allowed to drink. The bar is quiet—it's a Sunday and still quite early —so I have my pick of tables. I settle for one with a view of the Dubai fountain and ask for a wine list. Stress, I find, often calls for wine.

Sanjay walks in five minutes later and gives me a massive grin. I don't know if the grin is because a certain amount of fuckery has taken place in my life or if he is genuinely pleased to see me. I can see that he has his weekend look on. Instead of looking his usual can't-be-arsed self, he is currently clean shaven and his hair is gelled up. In fact, he looks quite dapper with his black shirt and blue jeans.

'I have a problem', I say when he has settled in and ordered a drink.

Sanjay raises an eyebrow. 'What's wrong?'

'My parents are trying to "arrange marriage" me.'

Sanjay laughs. 'No way!'

'Yes, way', I say, rolling my eyes, annoyed that he finds this funny. I briefly fill him in, including how determined my mum seems. Sanjay's met my mum. He understands that the woman means business.

He predictably gets straight to the point. 'Have you got a photo of the guy?'

I rustle through my purse for my phone and log into Facebook. The last search is still *Samar Grewal*. Sanjay peers closely at my screen with a hand on his chin, very obviously trying to hide a grin.

'Fucking hell, Alia', he says a few seconds later.

'What do you think?'

'Doesn't matter what *I* think, what do *you* think?'

'Well... I think he looks a bit disappointing, actually. Like, is this where my life comes to an end?'

He chuckles. 'Okay, marrying won't end your life.'

'It will end it as I know it', I argue, sounding alarmingly like a teenager.

'Okay, not gonna lie, you could do better', he says and leans back in his chair, still grinning.

I'm prevented from hitting him as I spot Meher walking swiftly toward us. I sigh with relief. Sanjay's unhelpful laughter will be balanced by Meher's sensible advice.

'Sorry I'm late!' she pants as she sits next to Sanjay. 'So, what's the hot goss?' she adds, running a hand through her black hair. I notice that she has made the effort to look nice with her red lipstick and black dress. There's no way Sanjay and I are the intended recipients of this look.

'My parents are trying to "arrange marriage" me', I say.

'Oh', Meher says after a brief pause.

'I'm not overreacting, am I? Getting into this arranged marriage situation is the worst thing in the world, isn't it?'

Meher purses her lips and stares at me for a few seconds. 'Is it?' she says.

'Is it not? I mean... Surely, at least after hunger, disease, global warming, loss of a loved one... Surely, after that, arranged marriage is the worst thing in the world, isn't it?'

Meher sits in silence with a pensive look as if really trying to think of something worse than arranged marriage.

'Not even then!?'

'Okay, it's not ideal', Meher starts. 'But what's the problem? Arranged marriage or the guy?'

'Both!' I sound notably more hysterical than I did a few moments ago. Why isn't she as outraged as I am? 'I'm not ready to be married. I'm not even thinking about a relationship. Imagine suddenly being pushed into this situation. How is it not the worst thing in the world?'

'But what's wrong with meeting the guy? If I were to set you up with someone, you'd meet him, wouldn't you? How is that any different to your parents setting you up with someone?'

'If you were to set me up with someone, I would assume it's for sexy purposes. If my parents are setting me up with someone, it's for child-bearing purposes. That's the difference.'

'Okay, think about this. When Bridget Jones's mother set her up with a stranger, it turned out to be Mark Darcy.'

'Balance of probability, though, he's more likely to be a Mr. Collins instead of a Mr. Darcy. Darcy doesn't exist, that's why he's been glorified in books.'

Will and Mark Darcy (unrelated) have been glorified in literature to the extent that that's what girls now want for themselves. Who wouldn't want a Darcy? Described as handsome through literature and then brought to life by the glorious Colin Firth. As if one adaptation in the nineties through *Pride and Prejudice* wasn't enough, he went ahead and did a second one in *Bridget Jones' Diary* and left us girls wanting more. When we wanted more, he obliged with a second and then a third Bridget Jones instalment and we still can't get enough. The idea of Darcy has been immortalised by Jane Austen and then again by Helen Fielding.

The obsession with Darcy is not uncalled for, but it has to be questioned. In the absence of his charming looks, he is just an arrogant sod who eventually realises that the woman in front of him isn't so bad. It happened with Elizabeth Bennet and it happened with Bridget Jones.

Do we really want an arrogant sod looking at us as if we've just said something utterly disgusting and then, realising his mistake, coming back to us? I don't even suppose that sort of attitude would work in this day and age. In an age of instant gratification, someone with that attitude gets swiped left immediately. Darcy would not be able to sustain himself in the modern dating era.

'Have you tried telling your parents you aren't ready to marry yet?' Meher asks.

I nod. 'I have. That doesn't seem to matter to them. They keep insisting that if I don't like him, I don't have to marry him, but that I should definitely go out with him.'

'Well, that's preposterous.'

'I know.' My teeth start to grit.

'Show her the picture, Alia,' Sanjay commands, clearly looking for another laugh.

I pull my phone out again and turn the screen toward Meher. She has the same expression on her face as Sanjay, but unlike Sanjay she doesn't laugh.

'Well', Meher says slowly, squinting her eyes a little, the apples of her cheeks rising up. She is obviously trying hard to find something nice to say. 'I don't mean to be rude, but... he isn't... all that, is he?'

'No', I say. 'I'm not being difficult, am I? I'm twenty-four, I'm not desperate to be married, he isn't my type, so I shouldn't have to settle.'

'I mean, you could still go out with him', Meher continues, handing me my phone back.

'I don't get it. If he was on a dating app, I'd have swiped left immediately, so why do I have to go out with him?'

Meher looks up. 'Why don't you just tell your parents that you don't want to go out with him?'

'I tried!'

'Well, then, it looks like you really don't have a choice.'

'Unless...' Sanjay looks up, his eyes gleaming in a light-bulb moment. 'Well, your parents can't make you go out with some-one if you already have a boyfriend. Why don't you just start dating someone else?'

'Oh, fuck that. Fuck that. Absolutely fucking not.'

'Why not?!'

'You know why!'

'You can't be serious! Not because of David!'

'Yes, because of David!'

'What?!' Meher is equally unconvinced about why I won't venture into the dating world. 'The guy from uni who ghosted you?'

'Hey! Being ghosted isn't nice!'

'It isn't, but you can't let it bother you so much! It's been a year. Alia, it's time to deal with your rejection issues.'

No, it's bloody not. I dismiss the thought of David and re-quest to change the subject. I don't want to be a downer while out with my two best friends. I want to feel happier things, like the joy of watching Meher slur after just one glass of wine, or Sanjay being a princess by virtue of not wanting to drink any tequila because he doesn't want a hangover the next morning to mess with his workout, and then promptly caving when I order it anyway.

We finally ask Meher why she's so dressed up and if she might be seeing a new beau. She says yes shyly, prompting a round of 'woohoo!' and 'waheyyy!' She refuses to give us details because she doesn't want to jinx it. I respect that although can't imagine ever shutting up about my new beau in the future when I'm over my trauma from the past. But maybe Meher is a level of mature that people like Sanjay and I can only aspire to be.

'Do your parents know?' I ask Meher.

She nods. 'Well, Mum does, but we'll keep it from Dad until I know whether or not I actually like him.'

'Can we at least know his name?'

'Akash.'

'And I presume you won't give us his last name?'

'No, I can't have you internet-stalk him.'

'I could just go into your followers and look up his name and find him, you know that, right?'

Meher pauses. 'Don't do that.'

Sanjay then proceeds to tell us how he technically really wants to be in a long-term relationship but also can't stop seeking out one-night stands. 'I'm so confused!' he cries. 'I want them all!'

'You aren't confused', Meher says. 'You're just a dick.'

'Why am I a dick? Why are men dicks for wanting just sex and being honest about it?'

'He has a point', I said. 'If he lured someone into his life with fake promises of a relationship, then he would be a dick. As he stands right now, he isn't a dick.'

Meher shrugs. 'Well, I guess casual relationships are beyond my understanding.'

'But'—I turn back to Sanjay—'I do hate that your parents would never bother you about getting married.'

'Yeah', Sanjay says with a grin. 'Well, I'm a guy. It's different for us, isn't it? I can imagine them getting on my case once I'm thirty, but luckily I have some time before then.'

'Yeah.' I sigh. 'Lucky bastard.'

'Yeah, I am lucky, I suppose.' Sanjay seems to be ruminating seriously. 'Dad has legit said to me this week that all I need to think about right now is doing a good job at work, whereas my sister gets regular shit from Mum and Dad about being single.'

'How old is she?'

'Twenty-six.'

Why Am I the Way That I Am?

As the week progresses and Mum and Dad seem to be getting more and more excited about the idea of marrying me off, I ponder Sanjay's suggestion to date someone new and thereby ward off the situation altogether. The mention of David opened up a can of worms in my head, though. Is Meher right? Do I now have rejection issues because of it?

David Preston and I were in the same year at uni and shared several seminars together. Coming from a life of never having been involved with guys except for digital poking, finding a clever and cute guy in the same year as me was like winning the lottery. We started chatting during seminars, and then after seminars. We started sharing songs on each other's Facebook walls. We started joining each other on club nights. We planned library sessions together and occasionally signed for each other at seminars if the other person slept through their alarm. The friendship turned into a massive crush for me, then blossomed into actual feelings of the heart as we spent more time together.

I spoke to several people about what I perceived to be a problem—having feelings for someone who I knew only thought of me as a friend—but nobody gave me a proper solution. Trisha said I should ask him out. Ask him out? What the fuck kind of shit advice is that? I have never asked anybody out, and the first person I go out with is not going to be someone I ask out. The first time I go out with someone has to be super romantic. He has to send me at least one handwritten note and our first kiss has to be at the Tower of London. Nothing less will do.

I then went to Sanjay and Meher. Sanjay laughed in my face and Meher looked at me with a smile. To Meher, the solution was simple: You like someone, you ask them out. If they say yes, you go out with them. If they say no, you move on. Life isn't as complicated as you make it out to be.

Sanjay, on the other hand, suggested something different. 'Have sex with him', he said. 'Use the condom you found in your welcome pack.'

Unhelpful, both pieces of advice. So I decided to go with my own idea and not do anything about it. If David fancied me, he would ask me out himself. If he didn't fancy me, maybe one day I would move on.

That lasted for nearly a year. A time period during which I never seriously dated anybody for fear of mentally cheating on David but never took it upon myself to let him know that I was holding out for him. I thought it would last forever, until the end of our final exams when David and I got super drunk and finally did what I had always thought we would never do. We had a sweaty, tipsy kiss in a club. We were not outside the Tower of London. We weren't tenderly holding each other's hands. We were clumsily holding on to each other for balance more than intimacy in a crowded club. Within minutes he asked me if I wanted to get a taxi home. I couldn't believe it was finally happening. I said yes.

And then we started dating. I couldn't believe it. After fancying him for so long, of imagining what it would feel like, of wondering what dating felt like, I no longer had to wonder or imagine. I was living the life I had only dared dream of.

It was everything I had ever imagined it would be. We got to know each other like we hadn't done before. It was strange, suddenly chilling with each other naked more often—of course we had never done that before and I had to actively ask myself not to giggle when around him in that scenario. It was also a little bit like teenagers sneaking out to see each other, because neither of us felt inclined to let our friends know that we were an item.

Then one weekend David went home to Bristol and came back a changed man. He became cold and didn't reply to my texts. I got ghosted by the first man I ever fancied, the first man I was ever involved with, the first man I trusted. We were good friends, almost best friends. When we started dating, we already knew everything there was to know about each other, except perhaps anatomically. If someone so close to me could end the relationship so abruptly and ghost me, could I really trust a stranger to respect me in ways that David clearly didn't? Could I really venture out into the dating world with no qualms?

One lesson stayed with me: Men are willies. Limp willies, incapable of doing anything except pissing about aimlessly. Never trust a willy.

In the year that followed, I didn't think about dating. I thought about David loads and with a lot of remorse, and I couldn't imagine ever wanting to be involved with someone again. But I know what it's like to really, really want someone. The knowledge of Samar's existence and my parents' intentions for the two of us against the backdrop of the existence of the Davids of the world makes me very nervous indeed, but can I really be blamed?

So Sanjay's idea that I should date someone just to get my parents off my back about Samar is as daunting as the idea of an arranged marriage.

Perhaps Meher's suggestion is the way forward, to just give the guy a chance. But I don't want to give him a chance. The ridiculousness of it all is that my parents will not take no for an answer, so although I ponder my friends' suggestions and my own qualms, the fact remains that no matter how much I protest, I will have to see the man.

For once in my life I do not look forward to a weekend.

Family Date

At what age do Indian parents go from being parents to re-
bellious teenagers who do exactly what you ask them not to?

This question has occupied my mind since Wednesday, the
day my father dropped a message on our family text chain to
say that the Grewals had confirmed dinner for Saturday night.

Dad: We'll all have dinner together so it's less awkward for you.

I stared at the message. Less awkward? Less *awkward*? Two
Indian families meeting for dinner to set their children up.
What part of that scenario is going to be less awkward than
me going out on a date with this guy? Has my father not met
Indian Aunties and Uncles? Does he not know how far away
they are from subtle?

But my parents won't budge. Anything I say will lead them to
think that I'm trying to get out of meeting the man. I do want
to get out of this situation but I'm more concerned about being
embarrassed at a family date. Imagine a person who isn't ready
to even think about dating getting thrust into a family date.
Imagine the parents then blatantly talking about marriage
and other stressful topics. Would that not make me want to
shit the bed out of anxiety?

So, reluctant as ever, I agree to meeting Samar at the family date. If only to avoid being typecast as the family's black sheep, I agree to come down to Abu Dhabi and listen to yet another lecture series delivered by my parents on why my marrying Samar is the best idea since sliced bread.

Every time they observe the slightest rolling of my eyes, my parents take it upon themselves to correct my thinking. 'Stop being so rigid in your thinking, Alia', Mum says. Or 'You should keep all your options open', Dad says.

They can't see the irony. They can't see that by depriving me of the opportunity to say no to Samar and exploring other opportunities, they are being what they are accusing me of being. Close-minded. Rigid. Set in their ways. Not even slightly open to the idea that perhaps I might want to meet someone on my own terms at a time deemed appropriate by me, who, after all, is the one who has to live with the consequences of this decision.

When I reach home on Saturday afternoon, my mother has already set out clothes for me. An asymmetric black top and blue jeans. She has also set out nude high-heeled shoes and left her own lipstick on my dresser because she thinks the red will bring out my 'fair skin'.

The last time my mother set out my clothes for me was when I was nine years old.

As I get dressed, my mother walks into my room and looks at me while I make that funny face all women make when applying mascara.

'You look nice.'

Shit. Why do I have to look nice today?

'Thanks.'

She sits down on my bed and I know what's coming. 'Alia', she begins. 'I know you don't want to do this. But this could be something special.'

I turn to look at her. 'I said I'll meet him. So I'm meeting him.'

'You keep saying he doesn't look great, but he doesn't look bad either. Looks don't last anyway. Do you think you'll look the way you do right now, thirty years from now? Do you think looks can provide a home, a livelihood, companionship, a family?'

I know looks can't provide a home, a livelihood, companionship, or a family. But they can provide attraction. Something. No? Surely, if there's no attraction, then there's nothing else either?

'I know looks aren't everything. And I'm not that shallow. I'm just not in the headspace for a relationship right now. You're making me do this, but I know what my answer is going to be.'

She shakes her head and sighs. 'Alia, why don't you understand?'

'I understand everything, Mother. I said I'll give him a chance. But if you're expecting me to meet him and instantly fall in love, well... fat chance of that happening. I'm going to need time. This is my life and I have to live with the consequences. Can you respect that?'

She nods quietly and sighs. 'Okay. You get ready, we'll leave in ten minutes. Trisha and Balveer will meet us at the restaurant.'

We set off for the Indian restaurant that my father has chosen as a safe bet where the chances of someone not enjoying the food are low. Trisha and Balveer arrive just as we enter, and once comfortably seated, Trisha asks if I want to split a bottle of wine.

'Sure, do they have malbec?' I say, peering at the drinks menu.

My mother clears her throat. 'Don't drink tonight', she says. 'What if they don't like girls drinking?'

'Samar drinks', I say. 'Remember his Facebook pictures?'

'Yes, but it's different for girls.'

Time travel is real and we have just gone back to India in the 1950s. So, as a woman I am expected to go through menstruation, PMT, childbirth at some point, a glass ceiling, mansplaining, catcalling in the middle of the street, ogling men, and I can't even have a drink? But Samar can?

From the corner of my eye I see Trisha shrug. 'Can I order a cocktail?' she says.

'Whatever you want. They aren't coming to see you, they're looking at Alia.'

Fantastic.

Ten minutes later, a group of three walks in. I recognise Samar from the pictures on Facebook and observe him as he walks in. He has on beige trousers, a blue shirt, matching blue turban, and a silver *kara* dangling from his wrist. His beard and moustache are trimmed and well kept.

He smiles awkwardly when he sees me, and it hits me that he too probably spent some time on my Facebook profile. He would have seen some confusing things. A video of me and Aisling doing a silly dance to "All I Want for Christmas Is You" to start with. A bunch of selfies from the gym. Another selfie with the caption 'I washed my hair today, can you tell?' and pictures from nights out with Sanjay and Meher. What would he have thought of me? Would he have thought me too silly for his taste? Ideally, yes, but men have been known to go out with women with cheesier captions and far more hip-happening parties. I can't be the worst he's come across.

The Grewals walk toward the table, the room now booming with the hearty sounds of men and women greeting each other with '*Satsriakal*[6]' and '*Ki Hal Chaal Ne*[7]?'

My parents introduce me to the Grewals. 'This is Alia, our younger daughter', and I fight the awkwardness I feel at being put on display. I smile at them and say, '*Satsriakal*' as demurely as possible.

Trisha is grinning beside me, no doubt revelling in my misery. I can't blame her. I did the exact same thing when Balveer's parents came to meet Trisha. The taste of my own medicine is proving to be quite bitter.

We sit down around the table. Bowls of popcorn and glasses of lemonade are brought in by the serving staff. Everybody looks at the menus while chit-chatting with each other. The waiter wants to take our orders, but everyone is busy catching up. Well, everyone except Samar and me. We are visibly uncomfortable, occasionally glancing at each other and smiling nervously, but not engaging in any conversation.

I wonder if it might be less awkward if I had a drink. Perhaps not. A few glasses of wine make me quite loud, and I wouldn't wish to inflict Loud Alia on anyone, not even an arranged marriage set-up.

'So,' Mr. Grewal says. 'Alia, what is it that you do, dear?'

6   Punjabi greeting
7   Punjabi for 'How are you?'

I look up at Samar's father and examine him for a second. His belly stands out from the rest of his being, and so does his hand which is holding what looks like a whiskey double. *How come he's allowed to drink?*

'I work for a research company', I say. 'It's called *The EMEA Bank*. We provide market intelligence, analysing political and economic risks in the Middle East and Europe.' I am aware that I sound like I'm reading my LinkedIn profile out loud, but engaging in conversation is a little challenging for me at present.

'Oh, that's very interesting', Mr. Grewal says. I chuckle inwardly. My own parents, to this day, don't fully understand what I studied at uni and what I do for a living and here this man is, so desperate to get his son wed that he is claiming he finds my line of work interesting.

Everybody looks at me as if expecting me to continue. I smile nervously, not sure what to say next.

'And what is it that you do, Samar?' I say finally, turning to look at the man of the hour.

He clears his throat. 'I am an auditor', he says and takes a sip of his lemonade. 'Tax auditor.'

Bond. James Bond.

Auditor. Tax auditor.

Sassy Alia is giggling away inside me. They have very different energies, Sassy Alia.

And very different personalities. Alia, you can't be serious about this. You could get a Bond. Don't settle for this man. I won't, of course. I just need to find a way out. *Open and honest conversation with your parents?* We've tried. *Have we? We sound like a teenager who wants to stay out late on a school night. Maybe we can talk to them about our qualms openly instead of just saying vaguely 'I'm not ready'.* Maybe. Yeah, maybe we could try that.

As we eat, it becomes evident that Samar and I do not excel at conversation with each other. Balveer steps in and asks Samar some questions about his life: How's work? Have you tried the kebabs here? They're quite delicious.

Turns out, Balveer runs out pretty quickly as well. Nice one, Balveer.

As the evening progresses, my nerves get a stronger grip on me. Why am I terrified? What am I terrified of? The right course of action is probably therapy, not an arranged marriage.

We get through the rest of the evening with no indication that Samar and I are interested in each other or even in having a conversation with each other. I say nothing to him, and he says nothing to me. That two people have been coerced into this awkward position could not be clearer.

And then it's time for dessert.

'What's everyone feeling for dessert?' Samar's mother asks as she browses through the menu.

'Would anyone like to share the banana pudding?' Mum says.

'Oh, I could go for that', Samar says. And then he does the unthinkable. He looks for a waiter and makes a distinct *shh-shh* sound to get his attention.

'Oh, my God, that's so rude', I say involuntarily. Everybody stares at me.

'Sorry?' Samar looks at me. 'What's rude?'

'That sound. You could just call out to him with words, you know?'

'It doesn't matter, Alia', Mum says through clenched teeth.

Samar smiles uncomfortably and places his order.

Dessert and a round of goodbyes later, we all bid each other goodnight, and I follow my family out of the restaurant in an awkward silence.

'What the hell was that?' my mother bellows. I am taken aback. I did literally nothing and this is the reaction I get?

'What?'

'You didn't talk to him! You didn't talk to anyone! The whole point of this dinner was for you to get to know each other and you just sat there tongue-tied. Such disrespectful behaviour, Alia. And then when you did speak to him, you were so rude!' She shakes her head.

'I- I was nervous', I stutter. 'And he *was* rude! He could have been more civil to the waiter.'

'Don't give me that.' She rolls her eyes. 'You knew full well what this meeting was about. How could you still be nervous?'

'In case you haven't realised, this is a massive deal for me', I say, rather hurt that my own mother fails to realise that marriage is a scary thing and the prospect—although only making me slightly nervous—should be making me shit the bed.

'Please, we have all been through it, what's so special about your case?' she continues. I turn to look at my father, who looks equally disappointed in me.

I turn to look at Trisha and Balveer, who are looking at each other intently.

'So, we'll go home now', Trisha says quietly and turns away in the direction of their car. Balveer bids us goodnight sheepishly and follows her.

'Mum, I'm sorry, I was just nervous', I repeat.

'Honestly, such a waste of time', she continues. 'We may as well have just not had this dinner if we knew you were going to behave this way.'

I feel embarrassed and frustrated in equal measure.

I never asked for the dinner party. I never asked to be set up. And yet here I am. Sure, it was probably not the best display of True Alia. True Alia is fun and makes jokes and teases Uncles and Aunties and that's why they love her, but can I really be blamed for not being my true self? Yes, most people go through marriage but why? Has anybody thought of an alternate lifestyle where instead of getting married, we fuck around and keep a dog for company?

'Alia', my father starts, turning the car ignition on. I hope he might say something supportive. 'That was very rude of you. They asked you questions and you gave one-word answers. What are they going to think of you now? You are a lovely girl but nobody got to see that because of your silly behaviour.'

I have nothing to say. A lone tear trickles down my cheek and I stare at the road ahead.

'Will you say something?' my mother snaps.

I sniff.

'Oh, great.' She rolls her eyes again. 'What did we say now?'

'Alia, there's no need to cry', my father says.

'We can't even talk to you. We say the tiniest bit of truth and the waterworks start. It's like we have to walk on eggshells around you.'

Clearly, my mother is having none of it.

'I'm sorry. I was just really nervous. You don't understand. I've never even been in a relationship, so of course marriage is a big thing.'

My parents sigh, almost in unison.

I understand where they are coming from. They want to be done with the responsibility of marrying off a daughter and they want to do it while they and I are still young. But, surely, given that I have to live with the consequences of a marriage, I should have a say in when I start seeing people for the express purpose of marital shenanigans.

We drive the rest of the way in silence, Mum and Dad lamenting having created a useless child, and me hoping for the next day to dawn sooner so I can head back to my Dubai life.

"I Do" but Not Really

An Indian mother is a dramatic mother.

Walking down the stairs the next morning, I am filled with dread at the thought of facing my mother, and I am exhausted. I stayed awake pretty much all night and when sleep finally came, it wasn't until about four o'clock in the morning. I don't mind. I'm going to head back to Dubai, where things might be less stressful and sleep might be more forthcoming.

I expect my mother to be red-eyed and looking exhausted herself, chopping onions for lunch. I hope she isn't. A red-eyed mother is a mother who has spent some time crying and is now likely to do some shouting.

In the kitchen, my mother is bent over the counter, chopping onions just as I had suspected. Luckily, though, she doesn't look like she's been crying. Unluckily, she looks pissed off.

'Good morning', I say.

She looks up. 'Morning', she says a second later and turns back to her onions as if nothing in the world matters more right now.

I can hear my father praying in the room next door. A few seconds later, he stops and there are shuffling noises. The door opens and he emerges, shutting the door behind him. He, too, looks pissed off. Great.

'Good morning, Alia', he says.

'Morning', I say tentatively.

The kitchen counter is lined with three bar stools and Mum has set out plates for breakfast. One plate is empty and the other has an egg, sunny-side up. I assume that I am not entitled to an egg.

'Did you want an egg?' Mum asks me with surprise.

'I'll make myself one, thanks', I say, walking toward the stove.

'Oh, sorry, I didn't know', she says. 'Let me make you one.'

'No, it's alright', I say and proceed to make my egg.

I once met a man off a dating app, whom I only ever knew as "Italian Man". His name sounded quite Italian and, not being proficient in Italian myself and also aware that he was not going to be that impactful in my life, I never bothered to learn his full name. For the purposes of the shenanigans we would be engaging in, "Italian Man" or even "Man" was quite enough. We met at a pub just outside Earl's Court station in London and then headed back to my flat. He claimed that he was going to break me, and I was ready to be broken. Two minutes later, as intact as ever, I realised that he had broken himself and that the night was coming to an end. As we lay together in my bed in total silence, I thought *This is awkward. This is awkward as arse. I want to leave but this is my home. I want him to leave.* I don't think I have ever felt more awkward about anything, ever, and I didn't think anything as awkward as that would ever happen again.

Wrong. That was one level of awkwardness. This, with my parents stewing in silence, is next level.

'So.' Dad finally cuts the tension in the room. 'Mr. Grewal said Samar liked you and wants to get in touch. Shall I give him your number?'

I look at him.

Is he fucking serious? We were awful! Sassy Alia sounds on the verge of hysteria. *Alia, no. Don't do this to me. There are so many things I haven't done yet. So many men I haven't fucked. Think about that list of nationalities we were going to have sex with, that list we made when we were sixteen. We only got to three or four!*

Is this a trick question? Do I actually have a choice?

'Okay', I hear myself say as Sassy Alia falls to the floor, clutching my leg, crying, begging me to change my mind. Sassy Alia can be a bit dramatic.

'Now, listen', Mum starts. 'You have to take this seriously. They are a nice family. Meet him a few times, get to know him. He might be something special.'

I nod quietly, focused on my egg like my life depends upon it.

Having agreed to do what my parents think best, the atmosphere at home lightens considerably. Dad and I joke around again, Mum offers to pack me a lunch to make amends for my lack of egg, and momentarily I forget what the future has in store for me.

When I get back to Dubai, I start thinking strategically.

Could I ghost Samar when he texts me? I can't, can I? His father would ask him 'So, what happened with Alia? Things going anywhere?' He would say 'Dunno, she never replied to me.' Mr. Grewal would say to my father, 'Your daughter didn't reply, is everything okay?' My father would then be super disappointed in me and I would be forced to deal with Samar anyway. No, ghosting could get messy and complicated, and that's not what one hopes to achieve through ghosting. Rather, complicated mess is an outcome that ghosting is meant to avoid altogether.

Oh, for fuck's sake, Alia, we can't even ghost in an arranged marriage; why have you agreed to do this? Shush, now, Sassy; working.

Could I be my worst self to him? Well, I was quiet for the entire evening this past weekend and he still wants to meet me. Apparently, my worst self isn't that off-putting.

Could I tell him something about myself that might intimidate him? Why am I not cleverer and more accomplished so I could just intimidate him out of my life?

I sigh. There's only one solution: actually meeting him and telling him the truth. If we can't do this through parents, it has to be done directly. But it has to end.

Matrimonial Sexting

When David asked me out for the first time after our accidental drunken sexual shenanigans, he was straightforward about it. He didn't booty call me again, but neither did he serenade me in a romantic way. Some might wonder why not, and they would have a point—why should a man not serenade me whilst asking me out? But I know the answer: It would cringe the shit out of my own existence, and dying of embarrassment from a romantic encounter was not how I envision my end.

So when David wished to ask me out in a romantic capacity, he sent a simple text.

David: Hey
Alia: Hey
David: Fancy a drink then? X
Alia: Go on, then x
David: See you at The Roebuck at 6-ish? X
Alia: Sounds good x

That was one way of doing it. Another way of doing it is how Samar Grewal has decided to do it.

Hello, dear Alia. Your father gave my father your number for matrimonial purpose.

Matrimonial purpose? If this is an attempt to make me cream my knickers, it is a disaster. Try harder next time. Or better yet, don't try anything.

I sigh.

Alia: Hello Samar

I put my phone away and turn back to my computer. Until receiving the text, the day had actually been going well at work. Well, I feel a bit silly to admit it, but a man of the eye candy variety was playing a massive role in how well the day was going.

As I walked into the office, I came face to face with a man I'd never seen before. A beautiful man. I asked him, rather confidently, 'May I help you?' Perhaps he was lost and I could help him find his way back. It was quite early and nobody, not even the receptionist, was in, so perhaps he had entered the wrong office. He could also be a thief, but he seemed too beautiful to belong to the criminal classes. He could be part of the maintenance staff, or the IT team; I knew we were expecting someone to come in to configure one of the new laptops.

'Oh, you must be one of the IT guys!' I exclaimed. 'There is one laptop to configure but I think my colleague Laura is on leave today.'

'I'm not an IT guy', he said with a frown. 'Who are *you*?'

'I beg your pardon?'

'Who are you and what are you doing in this office?'

'Um... I'm Alia. I'm the new research recruit?'

'Alia?'

'Yes.'

'That's the most Bollywood name I've ever heard.'

'What's your name, then?'

'Raj.'

I scoffed. 'And *my* name is the most Bollywood name you've ever heard?'

He chuckled. 'Name one Raj.'

'Uh... Raj Malhotra, Raj Babbar, Raj Kumar, Raj Kiran—'

'I said one!' His voice had risen slightly, but he was still smiling. 'Sorry, I should have known about you, but I just came back from holiday. I'm the Marketing Manager.'

'Ah, yes of course!'

'How are you finding things so far?'

'Yeah, good, thanks', I said, trying to ignore my cheeks that suddenly took to warming up. 'How was your holiday? Where did you go?'

'I went back home to Leeds for my sister's wedding. Not technically a holiday since it was a long and exhausting wedding', he added with a chuckle, 'but it was good to have some time off.'

A few minutes later I went to my desk and got myself a cup of coffee, unable to comprehend why the Universe would send me a gorgeous man at work. Up until that moment, I had never thought of a criterion I could assess men against, but looking at Raj made me realise that he was the criteria. He was... fit. Fucking hell.

His desk was to my diagonal left and I couldn't casually look in his direction. If he were to catch me looking at him, he would try to make conversation with me, and that was something I was decidedly against. Raj was eye candy. You do not initiate conversation with eye candy. You eye your eye candy. That's how the dynamic should be. When there are changes in the eye candy sphere, terrible things happen.

So, for the rest of the day, I found myself trying to sneak creepy glances at Raj. And now, as I re-read Samar's "matrimonial purpose" text, I feel my dream of having some eye candy shattering.

'Alia?' It's Mark, the head of the Research department. 'Do you have a minute?'

I freeze. I am not sure why, but anytime someone at work asks for a quick word, I'm convinced I am either about to receive a final warning or given the sack. That says something about the faith I have in my work.

'Yeah', I say coolly, hiding my internal panic.

We walk into one of the smaller meeting rooms that usually houses private meetings and my panic knows no bounds. If a budget cut is happening, I am definitely going to be fired because I am the new recruit still on probation. Well, that's just fab, isn't it?

We sit down across from each other and Mark smiles. We make slightly awkward chitchat for a minute before he gets to the point.

'So, how are you finding everything?' he says.

I raise my eyebrows. 'Good, thanks.'

'You've been here about a month now, and I think you've been catching on very well', he continues.

'Oh.' I sigh and smile. 'Not gonna lie, I did think you brought me in here to fire me.'

'No! Why do people think that?' He chuckles. 'No, I just wanted to check in to see if you were finding everything alright and if there was anything you needed from me.'

'No, I'm alright, actually, thanks. Aisling and Laura are taking care of me and I'm happy to be working with them.'

'That's great. There's just one other thing. Now that Raj is back, we need you to align your calendar with his social calendar. I've spoken to him, but just giving you a heads-up as well, it would be good for you to have a quarterly one-to-one with him. Obviously if you have any ad hoc changes, get in touch with him immediately and fix it, but quarterly is the rhythm we've seen working the best. Thoughts?'

I pause for a second, bursting with thoughts. Quarterly one-to-one with Raj. Ad hoc changes and meetings with Raj. Now I'm required to engage with eye candy?

Well, what did you expect? You work with the guy! Yes, Sassy, but I also work with Alec from Finance and how often do I speak to him? Literally three times since starting here.

'Yeah, that sounds good, I'll schedule that catch-up with him', I say.

Back at my desk, I find an email waiting in my inbox from Raj requesting a catch-up. The email is signed "R", which I find ridiculously personal. I don't mind it, but it's still personal. I reply to confirm that 10 o'clock the next day works fine for me.

Driving home, I ponder over what to wear the next day. Obviously, a one-to-one with Raj is not a date, but I do still wish to look super attractive. What will I even say to him? Well, he's done this before with the other researchers so he can lead the conversation. I just have to add my thoughts. What if I don't have any thoughts? What if I am so incompetent that I produce no thoughts of any significance whatsoever? No, that's silly. I have good thoughts. I am competent. I am clever. Really quite clever. I can do this. I will nail this. Raj is going to think of me as the best Research hire in the history of *The EMEA Bank*.

And as if the Universe can't stand me being positive for just one moment, my phone buzzes.

Samar: How's it going, Alia ji[8]?

I groan. Why must Samar be like this? He wasn't like this at dinner, so why is he being like this now? Who says *ji*? Seriously, why have Mum and Dad found me the weirdest of the lot? How do I tell them I don't want to see this man because he makes me cringe so hard?

Alia: Good, thanks, you?
Samar: Good, good. Listen, you wanna meet next weekend?
Alia: Are you coming down to Dubai?
Samar: No, your parents said you can come to Abu Dhabi

'Of course they did', I say under my breath.

Alia: Lol I haven't planned anything yet, but if I do, then why not.

8   'Ji' is a term often used to address someone older or someone in a senior position in India. Not so commonly used anywhere else so the fact that Samar used it is weird.

I open another chat on my phone—one with our family text chain—and type aggressively.

Alia: Mum, Dad, did we decide I was coming down to Abu Dhabi again this weekend?

Mum: Yes, we said you would come every weekend so you can meet Samar and get to know him. That is the only way this will progress.

Alia: Well, can he come to Dubai sometimes? Why do I have to come down all the time?

Dad: You can ask him to, there's no reason for you to have to commute every weekend.

I sigh. For fuck's sake. For real? This is my life now?

Working Not Wooing

Women have many things in common. The same frustrations about being subtly ridiculed at work by being mansplained to at every opportunity. The same irritation with men giving them uninvited tips on how to parallel park. The same question about whether one should wash their hair the night before an important event or wait until the day of. And the same doubts as to what to wear to look super sexy and super classy all at once.

How do I make this man believe that I am the best thing to happen to the Research department?

Sassy Alia scoffs and says *By being good at your job*, but I have decided to go down the superficial route. If you look the part, you become the part. So, if I look like I know what I'm doing, I will make people believe that I know what I'm doing. That was how I got through London anyway. Many a time people came up to me in Tube stations asking for directions, which surprised me because most of the time I was pretty lost myself. But I looked like I knew where I was going, and I can imagine that's what gave people the confidence to believe that I did know where I was going and could guide them where they needed to go. It's all about perspective.

I pick out a white silk shirt and a black pencil skirt. I tie up my hair in a ponytail. My glasses lend me the look of intellect that I hope will make Raj believe that I am the cleverest woman to walk the earth. I wear black closed-toe high heel shoes and set out for the office, ready to woo at my ten o'clock meeting with Raj.

I thought we're working and not wooing?

Sassy Alia is right, of course; I am primarily working but also slightly in the mood to woo. I am not going to attempt any flirtation with Raj, absolutely not. Male interaction for romance purposes has not been quite my bag since David, and I don't see that changing unless Raj turns out to be the most understanding, the most emotionally aware, and the most mature person ever. But I want him to notice me. Maybe it's human to want to be noticed, or maybe it's Nether Alia perking up to tell me that although I may have vowed to not date for as long as humanly possible, she does still have urges and might need some attention. So, for her sake, for the sanity of my nether region, I will attempt to get noticed by Raj.

The clock strikes ten and we make our way to the meeting room. Raj opens the door for me and waves me in politely. I smile and say 'Thank you' more flirtatiously than necessary. Sassy Alia rolls her eyes and I promise her not to do that again.

He asks me how I've been finding my role and the culture at *The EMEA Bank* and I tell him about all the challenges and opportunities I've faced in the past month. When he speaks, I find it hard to not stare at his mouth. I wonder what it would be like to run a hand through his beard. His lips look soft. He has a thick head of hair that looks just as silky as his beard.

You're properly lusting after him. Are you even listening to what he's saying?

I pay attention to Sassy and actively tune out Nether Alia's appreciation of Raj's looks. Then I start to pay attention to what he has to say about collaboration between our two departments and the importance of communication. I find it fascinating that he can speak for twenty minutes straight.

'So, basically', Raj says, brushing a hand through his hair, 'my issue with the other researchers has been that they write articles too close to deadlines and then we have to alter our social tiles. I don't mind if you do that; just don't add any new topics.'

'That makes sense.' I nod. 'Would it help if I sent you my plan for every issue about... eight weeks in advance? Would that help you put your comms plan in order?'

'Absolutely, that would be marvellous', he says with a smile. 'So, I think that's all from me. I'm going to send you the slide deck I put together for the others and you can just fill it in with your details and we'll take it from there. Do you have any questions for me?'

Yes. Do you have a girlfriend?

'No, I think I'm sorted for now.' I smile.

'Awesome. Where are you from?' he asks with a slight tilt to his head.

'Um, I grew up in Abu Dhabi, actually.'

'Yeah, I thought your accent sounded... different.'

'You can say weird. That's what everyone says.'

'No, it's... It isn't weird, it's quite lovely actually. Very neutral. I can't make fun of it.' He shrugs and grins.

I chuckle. 'How long have you been in Dubai then?'

'Three years next month.'

'Ah, and are you enjoying it?'

'Yes. I thought I'd stay here for two years, tops, and yet here I still am.'

'That's what invariably happens with everyone. Dubai sort of just sucks you into itself with its luxury and its weather and... beach days and brunches and whatnot.'

Raj chuckles. 'Yes, God, I never thought I'd be here.'

'What made you move?'

'Um, to be honest I'd become too much of a lad back in Leeds. Living the idle life. I didn't even have a job. I just thought the family business could sustain me.'

'What made you change your mind about... Well, not being a lad?'

'I woke up drunk on the cold floor in my bathroom at nine o'clock on a Tuesday morning. That's... Well, for a twenty-seven-year-old, that's not where I wanted to find myself on a Tuesday morning. What about you? What's your story?'

'Not very exciting at all, I'm afraid. I went to uni in London, my visa ran out, got a job in Dubai to get away from my parents and... here I am.'

Raj laughs. A glorious laugh. He's actually really easy to talk to, especially if I avoid looking directly at his face. We seem to connect. Conversation flows as we make jokes about being possibly an ethnic minority in the office. We talk about all things Punjabi and specifically British Punjabi. It feels like a breath of fresh air, being able to talk about my past life with someone new who would understand and appreciate elements of it. Of course, Sanjay and Meher have lived through that past life with me, but it's nice to be able to speak freely with Raj and have a laugh. It's a bit sad that the only other men I've been able to do this with are Sanjay and Balveer.

Raj seems like a nice man. Normal. Doesn't say things like 'Alia ji' or 'matrimonial purpose.' And he isn't a boring auditor. Tax auditor.

First Dates—Arranged Marriage Version

When I was younger, I'd imagine the best first date scenario. The man would ask me out, awkwardly, because his feelings for me get the better of him. I would say yes with a cheeky smile. He'd suggest an activity instead of a drink at the pub. I rather liked the idea of kayaking in Osterley Park then popping into the local cafe for a bite to eat and a drink. We would then walk around the park and, mesmerised by the beauty of Osterley House, we would hold hands and share a gentle kiss.

Now, at age twenty-four, I am going on a first date after a long time, with a man selected for me by my parents. This is no Osterley Park date. It is a date at the local Italian restaurant, a stone's throw from my parents' house. Strangely, the idea of my parents waiting at home, desperate to hear how the date went, is not the most effective mood-setter for a first date.

Very reluctantly, I agreed to come down to Abu Dhabi for the weekend. Mum and Dad insisted that I arrange to meet Samar twice during the weekend, to really get to know him. Luckily, Samar had plans Saturday night and so lunch on Sunday might be a better idea.

As I morosely get dressed, my mother appears and stands at my door. I know exactly what she wants to say but I'd rather she didn't because I already have that speech memorised.

'What time are you meant to leave?'

'Quarter to one.'

'Oh. Aren't you going to be late?' She looks around at my room, at the clothes scattered on the bed, the curling iron in my hand, and the towel on the floor.

'I'll be fine', I say with a smile, turning off the socket to which my curling iron is connected.

'Hmm.'

It's Sunday afternoon and I would like nothing more than to watch something on the telly and doze off. Instead, I am being made to socialise for romantic purposes. I gave up long ago on talking to my parents about how I feel, because I just get scoffed at. If I'm not going to be heard, what would I achieve by saying anything?

At a quarter to one, I leave the house. I have a distinctly "let's get this over with" attitude about this date, which is not how it should ever be. It's unfair to me and it's unfair to Samar. As I approach the restaurant, I wonder what it's like to be a white woman. If I were white, would my parents be this heavily involved in my love life? I highly doubt it. They might have hopes for my future, as my actual real-life brown parents do. But I doubt they'd be so heavily involved. This isn't anything against brown culture or white culture, but it is about individuality. One cannot deny that brown culture attaches massive significance to the family and the society—which is fine—but it ignores the individual. It's almost like focusing on "the greater good". We all know what happened in the *Harry Potter* books when

Dumbledore focused on the greater good. A bunch of muggles were killed. When Dumbledore's sister Ariana died because of this quest to fulfil the needs of the greater good, he realised that perhaps it wasn't worth the hype. Perhaps he should have focused on the individual.

My parents want me to date Samar because they perceive this to be the right time for me to settle down. And why do they think so? Because that's what's been happening for generations. 'We can't ignore the norms set by society', my mother says. 'The norms that have come to be, established themselves because they make sense', my father says. Sure, they make sense, but does that mean we can't experiment with other ways of life? Like staying single for as long as I need to? Not venturing out into the romantic world until I'm sure that my professional life is sorted? Or at least until I can learn not to shit the bed when I fancy someone? Surely these aren't the most radical ideas anyone has ever come up with.

I park outside the restaurant and sigh. *This is going to be a long fucking afternoon.*

Inside, I ask for the reservation under Grewal. The maitre d' leads me to my table, informing me that Samar isn't here yet. I sit down and the waiter hands me a menu. I'm starving so I take a look at the main course; there's going to be no faffing about with starters. Why do we do starters? Why do we tease our appetite with little portions of food and then get a large portion of food?

I look at my watch and then at the door, three times. Samar is late. Twenty minutes late. Should I text him? Would that make me seem more eager than I am? What if he has forgotten? Well, that's perfect. I get stood up, Mum and Dad take it personally, they sever all ties with the Grewals, and we needn't speak of this ever again.

Just then, Samar walks in. I involuntarily roll my eyes, but thankfully he doesn't notice.

'Hi', he says with a smile. 'Were you waiting for long?'

'Twenty minutes', I say with unintended iciness.

'What can I do, Indians are always late', he says with a hearty laugh.

I know not how to respond.

'So, how's your weekend been so far?' I say.

'Good.' He nods. 'I went out with some friends on Friday, and last night, so I'm a bit hungover right now. You?'

'Alright, thanks, I've been... Well, in Abu Dhabi... at home.' I am now cross with the Universe for giving Samar the opportunity to have a regular, hungover weekend like everyone else, while giving me a series of lectures from my parents about the significance of getting married at the right age. When I get up there, Universe, you and I are going to have some candid discussions about how you've basically been a bitch to me for no good reason.

Samar nods and we slide into an awkward silence.

He smiles and signals the waiter to come and take our order. When he leaves, we slide into another awkward silence.

'So, what do you do?' he asks me. I stare at him for a second.

'I'm a researcher.'

'Oh, yeah, you told me.'

'Yes.'

Samar nods.

What the actual fuck, Alia? I get that you don't want to do this, but does it have to be so awkward? You can't even speak to him? Could we cancel our order and just leave? I'd much rather go to a drive-thru Tim Horton's.

'What's tax auditing like?' I finally say.

'It's boring', he says with a tilt of his head. 'But it pays off my Lamborghini, so...'

Clearly, he doesn't know the art of subtlety. And he was late by twenty minutes and blamed it on an entire nationality. Why are we still enduring this?

I shoo away Sassy Alia and smile at him. 'Wow, congratulations on the Lamborghini.'

'Thanks.'

As our food arrives, my phone buzzes. The office group chat is currently brimming with messages. Raj has shared an article mentioning *The EMEA Bank*. The urge to send flirty texts to Raj strikes me but I control the urge because a) I'm at lunch with someone else, and b) Raj would be weirded out by the new hire.

Samar rolls his eyes at my food. 'I don't understand how people eat salads.'

'Are you rolling your eyes at my healthy decision?'

'Meals are supposed to be wholesome. What is that... leafy thing?'

'Meals can be anything you want, surely?'

'Yeah, but I need something meaty', he says, digging into his pepperoni pizza.

'Are you honestly judging me for eating a salad?' I ask him slowly.

'Yes.' He chuckles. 'That's rabbit food.'

'And your pizza is an illegitimate child of American and Italian cuisines. It's an abomination.'

'All I'm saying is, you're going to die regardless of what you eat, so you may as well enjoy your food.'

'What makes you think I don't enjoy my food?'

'You ordered a salad.'

'What makes you think I don't ever eat anything meaty—or wholesome as you put it?'

'Maybe you do.'

'Then why are you judging me?'

He pauses. 'I'm just joking.'

I finally give in and roll my eyes. 'This is the problem. People go around giving opinions on other people willy-nilly and then when they get confronted, suddenly they're only joking.'

'I *am* joking!' He chuckles uncomfortably. 'If you eat proper food on other days, why did you order a salad now?'

'Because I wanted a salad. I wanted some mozzarella, I wanted some basil, I wanted something refreshing. Why do I have to justify it to you?'

'You're being too serious', Samar says slowly. 'I was just making a joke.'

I look at him for a second. Then, 'Right.'

Later, when I recount the tale to my parents, they don't get nearly as cross.

'It sounds like you picked a fight for no reason', my mother says. She's fuming.

'What? Mother! He started it!'

'What did you find out about his family? His interests?'

I pause. So, Samar being a judgmental, patronising dickhead is clearly not a glaring enough red flag.

'He's got family in Amritsar.'

'And what does he do on weekends?'

'Well, he went drinking with his friends on Friday and Saturday. He told me he was hungover', I add, aware that drinking two nights in a row would make her question his behaviour a little bit.

'Oh', she says. 'He drinks that much?'

'Evidently.'

'Hmm, well... you go out drinking too.'

'Are you joking?' I chuckle. 'You didn't let me share a bottle of wine with Trisha when we went out for dinner, but his drinking is perfectly acceptable?'

'Do you not drink with your friends?'

'I do—'

'Then why can't he? What are these double standards?'

'WHAT ABOUT YOUR DOUBLE STANDARDS?'

My mother glares at me. 'Watch your tone, Alia.'

I sigh.

'What else did you find out? What did you think of him? Of his personality?'

'Mum, he was twenty minutes late. I was starving. He didn't even apologise. He just said that Indians are always late.'

'Hmm, not everyone is punctual.'

'Mum, he was... disagreeable', I say. I can't say 'dickhead' in front of her.

My mother purses her lips. 'Let's see. Alia, you can't disregard him after the first meeting.'

My father calls out to her and she walks away. I roll my eyes again, afraid that they're going to get stuck at the back of my head.

Many More Drinks Are Needed

Arranged marriage. It is perhaps a great business opportunity for pubs, bars, and restaurants with an alcohol license. When people are frustrated with their arranged marriage struggles, or any struggles really, they can head to a bar for a drink or three and find temporary relief from their woes.

When they get home, they aid food delivery services. I have ordered five shawarmas since getting into the arranged marriage turmoil myself.

When all the alcohol and shawarma starts to show up in weight and belly fat, people join the gym. This is one way for the fitness industry to thrive.

So, in a way, arranged marriage frustrations are keeping the business cycle alive. Keeping the economy afloat.

I take my personal responsibility to aid the growth of the economy quite seriously, so when I get back to Dubai, I hit up Sanjay and Meher to meet for more alcoholic beverages and more rants. This time, only Sanjay shows up because Meher has a date. With the same man. Akash. Here I am, struggling to not roll my eyes at every statement Samar makes, and there's Meher, voluntarily meeting the same man twice.

I wait for Sanjay in the outdoor seating area at one of the DIFC bars. It is nearing the end of November so the weather is quite agreeable. I don't exactly look like the girl my parents would be happy to see. My hair is in a messy bun that would appal my mother. I have in one hand a cigarette and in the other a glass of wine. The messy bun would be the least of her worries if she saw the cigarette.

'Well, well, well.' Sanjay grins as he walks toward me. 'I like this Alia because she lets me muck about, but I also don't like this Alia because she's clearly not doing so well.'

I smile. 'I'm alright, actually', I say.

'How are you, really?'

'Not too bad.'

'Then why do you look like a heartbroken Danielle Steel character right now?'

That gets him a chuckle. 'Well, I *am* a little bit pissed off, not gonna lie, but... overall, not too bad.'

Sanjay looks at me suspiciously for a second and then turns to look for a waiter. When one passes by he calls out and orders a beer and turns back to look at me.

'So, what's been happening? What have you been up to?'

It's a simple question but I fail to provide a simple answer. I unload on Sanjay. I tell him how going out with Samar has been hellish, about how he is basically the biggest prick I have ever known and how the Universe is being a bitch by not having Mum and Dad see the prick side to Samar. I tell him how the only joyous thing that has happened in the past few weeks is the eye candy in the form of Raj and that admiring him from afar is the only thing I look forward to during the day.

'If you're unhappy, just end it', Sanjay says.

'I want to. I will. I will. Just tell me how.'

'You could tell him you have a secret boyfriend.' Sanjay shrugs. 'Yeah! Tell him I'm your boyfriend. In fact, why don't I come along one day? You could introduce me as your secret boyfriend and he'll back right off.'

I stare at him.

'No', I say. 'That's too elaborate a lie and you'd have to come down to Abu Dhabi. Also, my parents know you and know we aren't dating.'

'Well, you won't like my other suggestion.'

'Anything is better than this plan.'

Sanjay purses his lips. 'Just tell him the truth. Tell him you aren't ready and if he has someone else on the horizon, he should pursue them. You'll chat to your parents when you're ready, but for now, you don't want this.'

'That's very Meher advice', I say after a second's pause.

'I know. I have to be the sensible one when she isn't around, clearly', he adds, glaring at my cigarette.

I purse my lips and then lean back in my chair, deep in thought about how simple and elegant his solution seems. There must be something very wrong with the solution that I can't see, but at the moment it looks like the only and the best solution available. Break up with him instead of having our families break up with each other.

I sigh. 'That makes sense. Ugh, I wish I was a guy! Or a white woman!'

Sanjay laughs. 'You want to be a guy?'

'When was the last time you had an argument with your parents about arranged marriage? When was the last time they set you up with someone?'

'Okay, yeah, we do have it easier, but trust me, it doesn't mean I don't face any pressure at all.'

'Does it not?'

'No, I face shit at work.'

'Oh, yeah, you probably do, being a lawyer and all that.' I nod. I always forget that he has a job with real responsibilities; it seems so outlandish. 'But that's professional shit. I would rather that than this.'

Sanjay shakes his head. 'The grass is always greener on the other side. You say that, but imagine actually having to work fourteen-hour days and waking up in the middle of the night because the Chicago office keeps fucking up.'

'Yeah', I say, nodding. 'That's true.'

'Having said that', Sanjay adds, 'I would rather that than an arranged marriage. Now, what's the deal with this Raj guy?' Sanjay picks up the pack of cigarettes and lights one for himself. I decide against commenting on his double standards.

'Oh, he's... just a crush.' I wave a hand to shoo away the thought of him being anything more than that.

'Have you got a picture?'

I show him a photo from Raj's Instagram and watch his expression change from a frown to a deeper frown.

'What's wrong?'

'He's alright.' Sanjay leans back. 'You could do better.'

'I'm not... doing him, per se', I say, locking my phone. 'Besides, by your logic, no one would be good enough for me.'

'And how far have things gone with Raj? Are you thinking of asking him out?'

'Oh, fuck no.'

'Why not? Not David again?'

'No, no, no.' I shake my head. 'Not David. It's just... we're colleagues. And there's absolutely no way that someone as fit as him is going to be interested in me. He's better as eye candy.'

'He's not that fit.'

'You're a guy. Trust me, if I show this photo to a girl, she'll feel the way I do.'

'I don't think so.' He shakes his head and then picks up my phone to look at the photos again. 'Really? This guy?'

'He's fit. You have to agree.'

'I don't see it. He looks like a fuckboy, honestly.'

'Oh, no, he's such a nice guy too.'

Sanjay chuckles. 'I know the type, trust me. They'll seem like the nicest of guys but they're fuckboys. I am willing to bet you... a hundred AED that this guy is just putting on a facade of being a nice guy.'

I stare at him for a second.

'I'll take that action', I say and shake his hand. 'Come to my work Christmas party. Meet him. Prove that he is a fuckboy and earn your hundred.'

'Deal.'

The End of the Arranged Marriage Road?

Dubai is not a Christmassy place. It can't be expected to be. It's hotter than the sun, for a start. Starbucks cafes across the city do not play Michael Buble. No one wants to snuggle under their duvet and drink hot chocolate while watching shit telly. But bless Dubai for trying. There are Christmas markets everywhere. Certain beach clubs transform into make-believe cinemas with massive projector screens showing *Home Alone*. And they serve mulled wine. And of course, Christmas trees pop up everywhere, including our office.

I have walked into the office this week, the first week of December, to the pleasant sight of the otherwise white and distinctly professional surroundings turning into a sort of Winter Wonderland. A large Christmas tree stands in Reception, surrounded by several small presents that people have been dropping off as part of Secret Santa, the reveal of which will be performed at our office party on a yacht. The reception deck has a bowl filled with Christmas lollipops instead of the usual toffees, and instead of the news, the telly propped up on the wall shows a YouTube playlist of Christmas songs.

"Last Christmas" by Wham! is playing on the big screen. I can't help but think about how every year I have thought of a different crush while listening to that song. Is this what the feminists fought for, being absorbed in thoughts of boys? I briefly think about Raj. The song doesn't really work. I didn't know Raj last Christmas. And I haven't given him my heart yet, so he hasn't had a chance to give it away yet. Complex philosophical stuff for a Monday morning.

As I walk toward my desk, my phone buzzes.

Samar: Hey howz u?

I stare at the message. Do I text now or later? How about I don't reply at all? He gets the hint, he stops texting me, we call the whole thing off and move on with our lives?

I look at the screen again. The *howz u* stares at me. Who types like that? Is he a child? Is he a teenage boy? Why am I being made to endure this?

Ughhhh for fuck's sake Alia, just ghost him.

Alia: Not too bad, thanks, how are you?

I lock my phone purposefully, as if not intending to look at it ever again, with a heavy sigh.

'That's a big sigh.'

I jump. 'Morning', I say to Raj with a smile that's probably far too eager.

'You alright?' He strokes my arm comfortingly. 'You look a bit peaky.'

'No, I'm fine, thanks', I say, still smiling. 'Just... an annoying text.'

You wanna go away together somewhere, Raj? You wanna fuck off, Alia? I thought you were supposed to be sassy. What is this Clingy Alia thing you've got going on?

Throughout the day, Samar tells me about the work he'll be doing in the coming week. I want to reply, *I don't care* but I don't. I think back to the date we had. I don't want to call it a date. I want to reserve the word "date" for any encounters where I actually fancy the guy. I think back to the spat we had because I couldn't take him or the things he says. I think back to when Trisha was dating Balveer and how he didn't say idiotic things that drove her mad. I resolve to end this.

Sanjay encouraged me to tell the truth. There is only one downside to that: I would have to tell my parents. Any attempt of mine to end this would be countered with several questions around whether I gave him a fair chance or not. At this stage, though, I have no more patience for Samar. If this was a dating app, I'd have swiped left a long time ago.

So I ask Samar if he is going to be free one of these days. Why prolong the agony? Let's meet sooner rather than later and get it over with. He says he'll be in Dubai tomorrow for work. Do I want to get a coffee after work? Yes, absolutely I want to get a coffee after work.

When my parents later enquire about my day, I tell them that a midweek meeting is booked with Samar. I think they take that to mean that things are going well, but I don't have the heart to put them right.

The next day rolls in and I am jittery with anticipation. I've never had to have this kind of conversation before. I have chosen a very open and well-lit place. Something dimly lit might suggest romance.

Samar walks in reasonably less unpunctual than before, and relatively smarter looking too.

So he is capable of looking and behaving nicely, but we just weren't deserving of it? Nice one.

I smile as he sits down, loosening his tie. 'How was your day?' I ask, aware that this is probably the nicest I have been to him. Maybe Mum is right; maybe I haven't given him a fair chance.

He judged you on your salad. Oh, yeah, no, he *is* a prick.

Samar tells me about his day and the meeting that brought him into Dubai, but I'm having trouble concentrating because I'm mentally rehearsing the words I carefully drafted with Sanjay's assistance.

'So, listen, Samar', I say, resting my hands on the table. As I do that, he leans in and I get a glimpse of what it would be like leaning in for intimate shenanigans with this man. I inwardly recoil. I lean back and clear my throat. 'The reason I asked to meet you today is... Well, I just wanted to be upfront with you and tell you exactly what I'm thinking so we can be on the same page... vis-a-vis... this thing.'

In my head, Sanjay is chuckling and Sassy Alia is rolling her eyes at how articulate I am.

'That's great', Samar says with his gummy smile. 'I appreciate anyone who is upfront.'

I nod with a smile. 'Samar, I'm not ready for marriage. I'm not even thinking about a relationship.'

His face drops. I feel a minor twinge of sympathy for him, but it's very minor because I could not possibly have misled him into thinking I was massively invested in "this thing".

'The reason I met you these past few weeks is, well, my parents. And I'm sure your parents put a certain amount of pressure on you too', I continue. 'So, I'm sorry for having wasted your time, but I really don't think I can continue seeing you.'

Samar nods.

'And if there's anyone else you're interested in, please feel free to pursue them', I finish, remembering Sanjay's advice to close all the doors and not let any doubts float in the air about potentially reconnecting in the future.

'Well, there's no one else', Samar says with a sigh. 'Or I wouldn't be here, you know?'

'Right.' I nod slowly. He hasn't finished his coffee. He hasn't even got through half of it. I should have timed it better. Now we have to sit and stew in awkwardness until he finishes.

'Well', he says, 'thanks for telling me. Yeah, my parents have been pushing me too, and... it's a nightmare, honestly.'

He looks up to find a waiter and makes that same *shh-shh* sound to get his attention. I flinch as I did the first time, and he notices.

'I don't have to change myself for you anymore', he says with a grin. He asks for a takeaway cup. Clearly, he doesn't want to stew in awkwardness either.

Oh, what a relief. It feels as if someone just lifted an immense weight off me. I can breathe again. I feel like my sinuses have cleared permanently. I feel like I could dance.

Arora v. Arora—
Decision Day

'Alia, come home tomorrow. We need to talk.'

I don't think any other sentence could make me shit bricks more.

'But it's Wednesday tomorrow,' I say quietly. 'Can't we just talk on the phone? Or wait until the weekend?'

'No', says Dad. 'Come home. You don't have to stay the night.'

A pregnant pause.

'Dad, is everything okay?'

Another pause.

'Yes. See you tomorrow.'

So, Mum and Dad want me to make the trip to Abu Dhabi and then drive back to Dubai. They won't tell me the reason, but I can make a few deductions. The invitation has come from my father instead of my mother, which means it's something serious. It has also come a day after I basically told Samar to fuck off and stay fucked off for life, although nicely and not in those words exactly.

As I head to Abu Dhabi, anxiety and nausea fill me to an extent I've never felt before. I'd asked Samar to keep it to himself until I could pluck up the courage to tell my parents.

'I know it's a big ask', I'd added. 'But just until this weekend if you could not tell your family, I'd really owe you one.'

'Yeah, of course', he said, and I'd walked out of there with a newfound respect for him. Could I have been wrong about him? I still wouldn't want to date him, but could he be less of a prick than I thought?

Now, however, given how cold Dad was on the phone, I'm starting to believe that trusting Samar to keep his word might have been a failure of my mental faculties. He might have gone home and expressed to his parents how I am the worst human being in all of history. Naturally, his parents would have had a word with my parents, thereby warranting this icy invitation.

Sassy Alia shakes her head and rolls her eyes. *You didn't think this through, did you?* When Sanj and I spoke, it made sense! *Since when does Sanj have a measurable sense of emotional awareness?* Fucking hell, what have I done?

'Hey!' I say chirpily when Mum answers the door.

'Hi', she says, less chirpily. Much less chirpily.

She moves aside to let me in and I see Dad watching the news on the telly. He doesn't look pleased. That could be due to the sorry state of affairs in the world or the sorry state of affairs in his own home.

'Hey, Dad.'

He turns to look at me, no smile on his face.

Fucking hell. We broke up with someone, we didn't kill them.

I sit on the sofa, ready to take the verbal bashing I know is coming.

It's sad, isn't it? Twenty-four and being yelled at by Mum and Dad?

'So', Dad says. 'What happened with Samar?'

Mum is seated quietly in a corner. Mum taking centre stage to chide me has been the norm since we were children, and I have come to prefer it that way. But Dad with disappointment all over his face makes this a hundred times worse. I've truly fucked up when Dad is disappointed. I say nothing because clearly he already knows everything there is to know.

Dad raises his eyebrows. 'Well?'

I swallow. 'I told him that I'm not ready to get married and I don't want to see him anymore.'

Mum sighs. Dad doesn't move.

'You couldn't tell us you were going to do that?' he says quietly.

I lower my gaze. Shame covers me.

'Now Mr. Grewal asks me, "if your daughter isn't ready for this, why did you ask her to meet Samar?" What do I say to him?'

Valid question, Dad.

I opt for diversionary tactics. 'Samar told his dad?!' I bellow. 'I told him that in confidence! I told him I needed time to talk to you!'

'It's not his fault', Dad says sternly. 'Mr. Grewal asked him what was going on and he came clean with them. Like you should have with us.'

'This is a joke, right?' I finally say with a sarcastic chuckle. Sassy and Real Life Alia have become one. 'This can't be news to you.'

'That is not the point, Alia', Dad snaps. 'If you were going to single-handedly end things with him, you should have told us. Now I look like the father who doesn't know what's going on in his child's head.'

I sigh, holding my head in my hands.

'I'm sorry I didn't tell you', I say. 'And I'm sorry it makes you look bad. But I am not sorry I ended it. It can't have been a surprise to you.'

I look up at Mum who has a frown on her face and Dad who looks more serious than I have ever seen him.

'You knew I didn't like him, and you knew I wasn't ready. You pushed me to it.'

'If you weren't ready', Mum says, 'you could have just told us. Why did you let us start this whole thing in the first place?'

I stare at her. She looks like she genuinely wants to know the answer.

'Are you being serious?' I finally explode. 'I told you from the off that I'm not interested! I told you after our date that he's a prick of the highest order! I literally said the words "I don't want to see him again" three times in front of you!'

'And we told you to give him a fair chance. Instead, you ended things.'

'Yes! Because it's *my* life!'

Mum sighs. 'When will you grow up and understand us?'

'No, I do understand you, which is why I agreed to do this in the first place. But you clearly don't understand me', I say, shaking my head. 'I don't understand what's so special about him that you would rather defend him than be on your daughter's side.' I reach over and grab my bag. 'Why don't you call me when you do understand me and don't think of me as an unreasonable drama queen?'

As I stand up, Mum looks at me. 'What, you're leaving?'

'At least have dinner', Dad says.

'No, there's nothing for us to talk about', I say. 'I know you don't want us to leave the house angry so I'm telling you this.

I am not angry. I just don't want to have the most awkward dinner of our lives while we aren't each other's biggest fans.'

Dad stares at me for a few seconds and nods. Mum looks at me and then at him, clearly not having it.

And that is the story of the first Indian woman to storm out in the middle of an arranged marriage argument.

Yeah, right.

Redemption

Nothing pisses me off more than traffic on my morning commute. It's too early to be on the road, anyway. Add to it the people who drive like idiots and should never have been awarded a driver's license in the first place and you have the recipe for Very Cranky Alia.

Although I can't honestly say that I can blame the roads and drivers for my mood this morning. I can't blame anyone. Maybe myself, a little? Can I blame myself? Yes, I think so.

I can blame myself for the drama I caused when I lied to my parents about Samar. Sanjay's advice was great, but my execution was poor. I have always maintained that I may not be the best-looking girl in the room, but I am quite clever and nobody can take that away from me. Yet somehow, I managed to be spectacularly stupid.

Mum and Dad won't talk to me. Can you believe that? After everything I went through with Samar: the bad date, the tardiness, the sense of humour that seems like a derivative of a 1950s patriarchal Utopia, the fact that I was never attracted to him, yet *they* are the ones refusing to talk to me.

Well, friends, the big lesson here is that lying is wrong.

I can entirely blame myself for the debacle. But I also want to blame Samar.

I never ask anybody for favours because I rarely trust people. For some reason, my small brain told me that I could trust Samar because he is probably in the same boat as me. My small brain was wrong. We are not in the same boat. We are not even in the same ocean.

Hang the fuck on, Alia. Sassy Alia, what? *If he had asked you not to say anything to your parents, would that have stopped you?* No, but I would have had the courtesy to ask my parents not to say anything to his parents. I would have told them that he asked me not to say anything. We would have understood! *You don't know that.*

Perhaps Sassy is right. Perhaps I don't know how I would have reacted if I was in his shoes. But I can't help but feel that life has been rather unfair to me.

I sigh and stare at the traffic ahead of me. The road is chock-a-block. It is not slow-moving traffic; it is stationary. In the distance, a car has been rear-ended by another, and a police car has pulled up next to them.

The car in the lane next to me is sliding closer to mine. I frown. Our cars are inches away. Perhaps he is paving the way to switch lanes when the traffic starts to move. Fair enough. He continues to slide and we are now centimetres away. Surely, he'll stop. He is now millimetres away. He is not stopping. I press the horn. I keep pressing the horn. The driver is alarmed. He rolls down his window. I roll down mine.

'What do you think you're doing?!' I bellow.

'I want to switch lanes. You don't have to honk so loudly!' he bellows back.

'You're about to hit my car, you prick!'

'I'm not an idiot, I won't hit your car!'

'You're literally touching my car, now back off! I am not having this! I have been stuck here for over twenty minutes, and I won't have you crash into my car. Back the fuck off!'

The driver is more alarmed than before. He rolls up the window and slips into reverse. I roll up my own window, suddenly aware that my heart rate is quite high and I am panting heavily. Damn, this is what rage feels like.

As the day progresses, Trisha continues to message the family text chain, apparently unaware of the family drama. When she doesn't get the usual banter from me and Dad, she messages me to ask if everything is okay. I say no, things aren't okay, and I am sick of it, of everything.

I keep my head down for the rest of the week and manage to not have any further road rage incidents. My phone is very silent; my parents' sulk has made me realise just how often we're in touch as a family. I miss their nonsense and bizarre use of emojis. Come Friday, though, it seems things are taking a turn for the better when my phone buzzes, announcing a call from Mum. With surprise and jubilance in equal measure, I answer.

'Hello?'

'Alia. Hello', she says courteously. 'How are you?'

'I'm fine, thanks, how are you?'

'Good.' I hear the faint presence of a smile there somewhere. 'If you're free this weekend, why don't you drive down to Abu Dhabi? I've asked Trisha and Balveer to come as well.'

It seems like anger is slowly seeping away to make room for civility, and civility could turn into love again.

I head home almost high on the knowledge that despite the spat, Samar is truly a thing of the past and my family will be mine once again, unconditionally.

Dad sits us all down and tells us that Samar is now engaged. Yes. Engaged. To be wed. Engaged to his long-term girlfriend. Yes. Long term. They were on and off for a few years. They'd hit a few bumps along the way, like when she was cheating on him with a guy she went to uni with, and like the time he started seeing me. But true love has prevailed and marriage is coming to town. Six months hence, 'Samar weds Rania' will take place in all its glory at the Emirates Palace Hotel. We are all invited.

When Dad finishes his announcement, I smile and RSVP no. I don't know what else to say, so I let my grin do the talking. "I told you so" is not really my style, you see. Yes, I could point out the prick nature of Samar, or I could let it slide. There is a certain class in letting some things slide. And I am quite sure that by incessantly smiling, I am saying it best by saying nothing at all.

Trisha is outraged. 'If he had a girlfriend this whole time, what was all that about? Did you just torture Alia for no reason?' she bellows. I continue to smile as my mother shrugs.

Dinner goes by in peace. Well, internal peace. Externally, Trisha and Balveer are still outraged, but I thoroughly enjoy myself. It feels like I have earned enough ammunition to last the rest of my life. Any time my parents come up with another bright idea like this, I can just use Samar, the failed experiment in matrimony, as a reason why this should never be attempted again.

In my heart it feels like the calm after a storm. We talk about the calm before a storm. We fear the calm before a storm. But there is something to be said about the calm after the storm. You can see the destruction. But you can also see the relief.

You know things can't get much worse and that up is the only way to go. I love that.

In this new calm after the storm, there is a renewed love and connection in the room. We enjoy Mum's cooking like we had never done before. Trisha and I drain the bottle of wine and talk about life as we knew it without the likes of Samar. Dad and I join forces to crack the worst Dad jokes in history and Mum rolls her eyes at us before laughing and shaking her head.

I think about Sanjay and how his advice set me free. Sassy Alia internally apologises for thinking Sanjay didn't have a measurable sense of emotional awareness. I think about Samar and Rania and how they had been cheating on each other before ending up with each other. Is that what relationships are like? Do people often meander over to other paramours for shits and giggles, or are Samar and Rania just excessively toxic? If Samar truly is that toxic, and I have indeed just dodged a bullet, should I be thanking the Universe, the snarky little bitch? The world truly works in mysterious ways.

The Perfect Week

Knowing that next weekend won't be spent with Samar or field-ing questions from my parents makes the week more enjoyable than I could have imagined. Maybe this is what appreciating what you have feels like. Isn't that what people say? That sad-ness comes so that you can appreciate happiness more?

That is the most ridiculous thing I have ever heard.

On Monday, I waltz into work all dressed up. I have on a work-appropriate red bodycon dress and leopard-print heels because this Samar-free world makes me feel bold. Everybody says that I look nice. Raj says, 'You look... bangin'.'

Obviously, I overthink that. Raj has a lad background—well, if Sanjay is to be believed—and so saying something like "you look bangin'" is probably just his way of speaking. But I am me and I overthink to the point of nearly dying of anxiety. Additionally, Sanjay has cast doubts into my head about the authenticity of Raj's "nice guy" persona, so using the word bangin' in any context raises many questions.

I have another one-to-one with Raj where he tells me more about his family and the lad life he left behind in England. We talk about the UK Bhangra scene, reminisce about clubs in England that we both frequented, and lament over the state of world politics.

'There's a chance we bumped into each other on one of those nights at Gatecrasher', Raj says with a small smile.

I nod. 'Yes, there is.'

'Although, I would have remembered you.'

'Yeah?'

'Yeah. I mean... not to sound work-inappropriate, but you'd have been exactly my type.'

'And what was your type?'

'Someone hot', he says with a chuckle.

I laugh. *Are we hot, Alia? Is that what he's saying?* 'And what's your type now?'

'Um... confident, worldly... and I wouldn't mind if she was a looker.'

'Mm.' I nod again. 'Well, if we had bumped into each other, I don't think I would have looked at you twice', I say with a small grin.

Are we... flirting?

When it's time to go home, I still need to send a few emails, so I bid everyone goodbye and give myself another half an hour to finish my work for the day.

'See, this is what happens when you spend the day slacking', Raj says and waves me goodbye with a grin and a wink. A wink. What the fuck does that mean? Is he or is he not flirting? And what has brought this on? Is he going to transform into a fuck-boy? Am I losing a hundred AED?

On Tuesday, Raj follows me on Instagram. And likes a few of my pictures. Two of them are recent. One is from a year ago.

On Wednesday, Raj sends me a meme on Instagram. I send him a "rolling on the floor laughing" emoji. An hour later he sends me another meme and I catch him looking at me from his desk. I grin and open the app again—and laugh.

'That's funny, eh?' he says and I nod, continuing to laugh.

Laura and Aisling look back and forth at us. 'What are you two giggling about?'

On Thursday, Raj asks me if I would like to get a drink at the Spanish bar downstairs.

'An ex-colleague is visiting. I think you two would get along', he says with a smile.

Hang on. 'Get along' as in, is he setting us up with this guy? I have absolutely no idea. Why does he even want to take us? *I reckon it's the red dress.* Or, you know, I'm hilarious. *Nah, it's the dress. You have no personality.* Just once, I wish you'd be on my side.

I say yes to the drink.

We head down to the bar where happy hour is happening. Which means I could get shitfaced in exchange for a smaller than usual amount of money. The ecstasy of spending less money than usual will prompt me to get even more drinks and I will end up spending the same amount of money or even more.

We order our drinks and within minutes, a tall and lean man with dark hair and a Mediterranean face walks toward our table.

'Bernie!' Raj says with a broad smile. I ignore the little butterflies in my stomach that flutter every time I see him smile.

Bernie smiles at me and shakes Raj's hand. 'Hello', he says to me, extending his hand forward.

'This is Alia', Raj says, as I shake his hand with a smile.

'*You're* Alia?' Bernie says, raising his eyebrows with a grin.

'Have you guys been talking about me?' I say slowly, looking from Bernie to Raj and then back at Bernie.

'He was just telling me about who replaced me.'

'Oh, am I doing your job?!'

He nods. 'Yes, I was in charge of the Middle East until a few months ago.'

'I had a feeling Raj had a problem with me', I say pointedly. 'The first time we met, he thought I was an intruder. And now the first chance he gets, he's bitching about me to his ex-colleague', I add with a small grin.

Are you flirting? It's pathetic.

'Ah, he's a bad colleague, no?' Bernie says.

'That was a mistake!' Raj says, waving his hands. 'I apologised! And I bought you a coffee!'

Bernie and I chuckle.

'So, what are you doing now, Bernie?' I say.

'Nothing for now. I'm heading back to Spain to be with my girlfriend', he adds wistfully.

Ah. So, he wasn't trying to set us up with him. Then what's his game here? Maybe he's just being a nice colleague and getting to know us.

We continue to chat about Bernie's experience at *The EMEA Bank* and how after years in Dubai he realised it was time to go home. I wonder if that is what happens to everyone; there's a moment of truth when they realise that their time in this glamorous, surreal city is up.

A few rounds of alcohol later, I am starting to slur and my body feels like jelly.

'I think I'm gonna head home', I say to Raj over the loud music playing in the background. 'Where's Bernie?'

'He's just gone to the bathroom', Raj says, moving closer so I can hear him. I have a strong urge to grab his face and kiss him. I resist. 'Why do you have to leave?'

'Because', I say, staring at him with wide eyes, trying to focus, 'I'm a lil' bit drunk.'

Raj grins. 'Good', he says.

I chuckle.

'It's nice to see you outside of work', he says, also speaking louder than normal. 'You look nice, by the way', he adds.

'Thank you!' I yell, smiling.

What is happening? Do you think he fancies us? I don't know, maybe? *Ugh, I think he might be too keen. This is a bit icky. I've got the ick.* Are you joking? *He's being too nice. We need a fuck-boy.* WHAT?! Are you *fucking* joking?!

Another round later, I feel ever closer to throwing up. I look at my phone: it's half past ten. If I go home now, I can go with my dignity intact. I can drink some water, remove my makeup, and maybe even take some paracetamol to prevent a headache.

I look up from my phone, determined not to throw up in front of a man I fancy and who, miraculously, seems to be flirting with me. This never happens. I usually gather the attention of creeps and men considerably older than me. I am not about to ruin this by throwing up in front of him. I order myself a safe driver. If I leave now, I leave him wanting more. If I throw up, I leave him wanting more of someone else, anyone else.

The driver gets to the bar within fifteen minutes and I bid goodbye to Raj and Bernie.

'I still think you should stay,' Raj says to me. He turns to look at Bernie. 'Don't you?'

'Yes, absolutely!'

'If I don't leave, you guys won't be able to talk about me again', I say, still slurring but still confident.

Raj smiles. Then, 'Come, I'll walk you out.'

'I get that you're a gentleman, but the door is literally right here.'

Bernie chuckles.

'Come on', Raj says with a sigh and grabs my arm by the wrist.

At the door, Raj smiles and leans in. For a second, my heart is caught in my throat. He slides to a side and hugs me, one hand resting on my waist. I feel like he kisses me on the cheek but I can't be too sure.

The lift arrives and I walk in. As the doors close, I have a sudden vision of him walking in with me and kissing me like there's no tomorrow. I suddenly wish I'm Raven from *That's So Raven*, my drunk mind desperately wishing for the vision to become a reality.

In the car I unlock my phone. There are a few messages from Meher, planning a weekend soiree of wine and food. I RSVP yes. There's one from a client, asking for a rewrite. And then my phone buzzes to another message. It's from Raj.

Text me when you're home x

I smile slowly, resisting the urge to reply with *Why? You're not my mother.*

Friday is a day of celebration and remarkably low productivity. The end-of-week catch-up is stale in comparison to the Monday catch-up. Today we only talked about our work Christmas party. I like Christmas and I like to party. The company has booked a yacht from seven until eleven o'clock on the Friday before everyone leaves for the Christmas holidays. We have three weeks until that day, and the question we're faced with is quite daunting: Will you be bringing a plus one? Let us know by the end of next week so we can confirm numbers.

'You bringing someone then?' I hear Aisling behind me.

I turn to look at her. 'Yes, my friend Sanjay', I say with a nod.

'Ooh, a friend?' Aisling grins. 'Is this a friend-friend, or a... boyfriend?'

'A friend-friend', I say firmly.

'Are you not seeing anyone then?'

'Nope.' I shake my head, briefly thinking about Samar and internally cringing.

'What about you, Raj?' Aisling says. 'Are you bringing a mysterious friend to the party too?'

'He's not a mysterious friend, he's literally just a friend!' The last thing I want Raj to assume is that Sanjay is a boyfriend. It would be like I was dating my brother. Yuck.

'Um', he starts with a smile. 'No, no mysterious friends for me.'

I smile at him and watch him walk away. Raj is single for the foreseeable future—that's what I like to hear. I'm not sure what I will do with that information. I have no intention of "getting any" from him, but knowing that nobody else is getting any from him either is quite satisfying. It's like I'm not eating my cake and not having it either.

Not a Good Idea

Being overly enthusiastic at Christmas is one of my favourite things to do. I'm not the only one. One day, as part of the collective office slacking, every time the receptionist answered the phone with 'Buddy the Elf, what's your favourite colour?' Raj gave her 50 AED. She ended up earning 200 AED.

The most Christmassy day at the office dawns as we get closer to the 25th. The day of the Christmas party. We are all at the office to start the day and exchange Secret Santa presents, and work is the last thing on anyone's mind. We come in at nine o'clock and check emails for an hour, after which point, carol singers throng the building and everybody gets sucked into a Christmas black hole powered by Michael Buble and Father Christmas.

It truly is a merry time as we unwrap our presents and find that they match our wish list exactly. I ended up buying a portable blender for Aisling and my Secret Santa ended up buying me a gift card to the salon downstairs for a facial. I like to pamper myself, but it's better when someone else sponsors it.

As lunch time approaches it's evident that nobody is in the mood to work or even pretend to work. An executive decision is made, and we leave the office at two o'clock. This is great; it gives me the opportunity for a nap before I have to get dressed for the boat party, which I am ridiculously excited about. The boat party is going to house most of my favourite things in the world:

1. A boat. I love boats.
2. A bangin' playlist. Love a good tune to jam to.
3. Sanjay. He's kind of annoying sometimes but I love him to bits.
4. Raj. Enough said.
5. Prosecco. Because why not?
6. Shawarma platters. Best food known to mankind.
7. A direct view of the Atlantis Hotel on the Palm. It is a spectacle beyond comparison. To a tourist this would seem like paradise, but even to a resident, the beauty never ceases to amaze.

I get dressed and wait for Sanjay to get to my flat for pre-drinks. The difference between pre-drinks with female friends and pre-drinks with male friends really amuses me. Pre-drinks with Sanjay usually means a bottle of vodka and watching random YouTube videos. Pre-drinks with Sanjay and Meher means calculated drinking where Meher ensures we drink enough water between alcoholic beverages.

'Meher, you do realise the point of pre-drinking is to ensure we're well drunk before we get to the venue, don't you?' Sanjay would ask, staring cautiously at his glass of water. 'Why are we sobering down?'

'So you don't throw up outside the club like Alia did on Broad Street', Meher would say, looking at me with a raised eyebrow, rubbing in the cringe-worthy memory of boozy nights out in England.

Now, however, things are slightly different. The bottle of vodka does sit between us, but the YouTube videos have been replaced by conversation.

'Any hot girls in your office?' Sanjay says, pouring out the liquor into two glasses.

'Yes. There's a Romanian girl who isn't looking for anything serious, so you two might get along. There's also an Indonesian girl.'

'Oh, cool, I've never had Indonesian before.'

I cringe. 'I can't believe you're coming along to stalk Raj to see if he's a decent guy when you talk like that about women!'

Sanjay chuckles. 'You know I'm joking!'

'No! This is why I didn't like Samar! You can't just say shit and then cover it up with an "I'm only joking". Say you're sorry!'

'Fine, I'm sorry', Sanjay says with a smile. 'But congratulations on finally ending things with Samar.'

'Why, thank you very much', I say, beaming. 'It's Christmas and I don't have a dumbass in my life, and somehow it's thanks to you!'

Sanjay laughs. 'That's the shittest thanks you've ever given me.'

'No, but seriously', I say. 'That was great of you, having my back, listening to my problems, even giving me advice I could follow. Thank you.'

'No worries.'

We reminisce about the peaks of our friendship, like the time I pulled an all-nighter with him at the library while he worked on his dissertation, to help him with his citations, or when he spent three months in a toxic relationship with a girl who was consistently cheating on him and I broke up with the girl on his behalf so she couldn't beg him to take her back for the millionth time. We briefly talk about Meher, who declined another invitation to hang out with us because she was out doing adult things like getting to know a man better. We couldn't blame her; she has seen plenty of Sanjay and me in drinking action and probably could do with mature conversation (assuming Akash can match her).

Sufficiently tipsy, we make our way to the Marina harbour. Sanjay has his eyes peeled for any fuckboy behaviour Raj might exhibit. He introduces himself to Raj almost curtly and Raj's half smile makes it evident that he doesn't understand Sanjay's animosity. I roll my eyes at how unnecessary this all is.

'It isn't unnecessary at all', Sanjay says when I drag him to a corner. 'You're crushing hard on this guy and as your best friend it's my job to ensure you don't get entirely fucked by him.'

'Nothing is going to happen! I'm not even looking to date him. Please, just enjoy the party. Let's call off the bet.'

Sanjay chuckles. 'Scared of losing a hundred AED?'

I roll my eyes yet again. 'Come, I'll introduce you to those girls.'

It is soon time to board the yacht and everybody is quite taken in by the glamour. We climb up to the top deck and almost simultaneously everyone wants a picture against the backdrop of Pier 7. I shake my head. *Amateurs*, I think. *There's going to be more fabulous views once we start.*

In true Dubai spirit, it is the most unusual Christmas party, but it is, as Aisling claims, 'fancy af'.

Soon enough, the music takes control and the scene reminds me of a club night from university where the brown kids (I can call them brown because I'm brown too) would sway like wiper blades to the sound of RnB and the white kids would perform cheesy moves to "Mysterious Girl" by Peter Andre. And like every party, Punjabi MC's "Mundian to Bachke[9]" comes on and the cries of 'Raj!' and 'Alia!' are loud enough to prompt us to do our duty to the global Punjabi population and perform Bhangra moves to the song. I drag Sanjay into the dance-off too, and I can see that he and Raj are now cheering each other on. When the song ends, they start chatting to one another. I smile. Perhaps Sanjay might let the bet go.

Later, I sit next to Sanjay. 'So, what do you think of Raj? Does he seem like a fuckboy to you?' I take a large gulp of gin and tonic.

'No, he's alright, actually', Sanjay admits. 'Maybe I didn't need to supervise.'

'Nah, it's good to have you here. I can't make any Punjabi jokes in front of white colleagues, they don't get them.'

Sanjay chuckles and we drink in silence.

Then, 'hey', I say, 'have you got a lighter?'

'Fucking hell, Alia', he groans. 'Stop smoking!' He reaches into his pockets and retrieves a lighter. 'This is the lighter I stole from you before we left. I'm giving you this if you promise you'll stop after this.'

I grin. 'Okay, New Year's resolution, I quit smoking.'

'You and I both know you don't believe in New Year's resolutions.'

9   The song that DJs play to identify the Punjabis in the party. Seriously, YouTube it, you'll know which one I mean.

'Fine, I'll smoke downstairs then', I say, standing up.

I reach out for the rail by the steps that lead downstairs. It's narrow and barely qualifies as a staircase given that it's only five steps. It winds down onto the lower deck, where I see Raj texting. He looks up and smiles.

'What are you doing here by yourself?' I say, taking the cigarette out of my mouth.

'Oh, just texting my mum', Raj says, locking his phone. 'I leave tomorrow and she wants to know what time I land.'

'Ah, that's right, you're leaving', I say, pretending I haven't been thinking about how lonely the office will be in his absence. 'Are you excited?'

'Yeah', he says. 'It's been ages since I saw them all.'

I continue to smile and he looks at me for a few seconds. In an attempt to cover the awkwardness, I shift my attention to the lighting of my cigarette.

'I didn't know you smoked', he says slowly.

'I... Well, it comes and goes', I say with a small roll of my eyes. I could tell him about how the Samar situation prompted me to turn to alcoholism and tobacco, but that could take a while to cover.

'Right', he nods. 'Well, I just feel... someone as beautiful as you shouldn't smoke.'

Now, at this point I am quite tipsy so there are multiple reactions in my head.

There's Sassy Alia laughing. *What? What a line! Hahahaha.*

There's Tipsy Alia grinning and trying to make me lean forward and touch his face and grab his hair.

And there's Real Life Alia, i.e., the Alia that people see, who is speechless and staring at Raj with wide eyes.

I blink a few times and drop my cigarette into the water. Without a word Raj leans in closer. I lower my gaze as shyness takes over, but I can also hear laughing. I wish I could shoo Sassy Alia away, but she lives in my head rent-free.

As Raj kisses me softly, though, all the Alias unite to become one and the laughter ceases. I feel his hands reaching for my waist and I feel my own hands reaching for his beard. I smile inwardly thinking about how long I've wanted to touch that beard.

My heart rate seems to have increased considerably. I seem to be breathing heavily and my skin seems to be more sensitive. It's been a long, long time since I've felt this way and I don't want it to end.

And just as quickly as it registers in my head that we are indeed kissing, Raj says one of the least sexy things any man has ever said to me.

'Alia, I think we should go back inside.'

Over the years, men have said some truly horrific things. Here are the top five worst things to say post-sexy times:

5. I think we should go back inside (immediate regret, I like that)
4. I've just got out of a serious relationship so I want to spend some time getting to know you before anything happens between us (from a very handsome Italian man I'd met on a boat, whom I was definitely not going to spend a lot of time getting to know)
3. We are not having sex tonight (gee, thanks for coming up to my flat then)
2. I think I'm going to be sick (unrelated to me, the guy had been drinking loads before we kissed)

1. I don't want you to get into shit with your parents, so I'll take you home (reminded me of my parents and I didn't get any—massive de-rection)

I nod vigorously and follow Raj toward the stairs. However, my drunk brain has something else in mind. I reach out to his shoulder and stop him.

'Why?' I say.

Raj turns to look at me and sighs. 'Alia, we've both had a lot to drink, and this wasn't a good idea. I shouldn't have kissed you.'

'Okay, but', I say. 'I like you even when I'm sober.'

Raj looks at me with a face that's hard to read. Is he happy? Is he cringing? I can't tell.

'I can't do this', he says slowly. 'I'm sorry, I should never have done this. I blame your dress', he adds sheepishly.

I am not amused.

'Let's go back inside', he says.

So, the joy and peace I'd been feeling before the kiss was the calm before the storm.

(Not a) F*ckboy

Dictionary.com's definition of a fuckboy:

In 2017, a fuckboy is someone who doesn't respect women, is a player who won't commit, and is basic in his clothing choices and personality.

Raj didn't disrespect me. He apologised to me. He didn't commit to me, but he didn't mislead me either. He is not basic in his clothing choices or personality. He is actually quite well dressed.

I didn't lose 100 AED to Sanjay because the bet was that Raj would be a fuckboy. I may as well have given him the 100 AED though, because despite not losing the bet, I did lose my dignity a little bit. I thought I'd lost it a long time ago, but turns out the smithereens that I had left, I gave away to the Universe when I decided that telling my colleague that I fancied him sober was a good decision.

Should I be given adult privileges like drinking alcohol? Am I truly mature enough? Why do we continue pouring shots of tequila when we know that every single time we've done that in the past it has led to mistakes?

After we get off the boat, Sanjay and I walk over from the Marina harbour to get post-alcohol greasy disgusting food. We end up at a restaurant that describes itself as an authentic British chip shop, with authentic Dubai high end–restaurant prices.

'Eighty AED for a doner, are you serious?' Sanjay says, flipping the menu over.

'It's authentic British doner', I say slowly.

'Doner is Turkish!' Sanjay says. He's clearly less drunk than I am.

'My treat.' I smile. 'I owe you for the bet anyway', I add flatly.

'Stop that, that's silly', he says. 'If it helps, he doesn't seem like a fuckboy so technically neither of us won.'

No, Raj doesn't seem like a fuckboy, but I do seem like the overly keen and overly enthusiastic child who just spilled the beans on her own silly little crush. Is this the Universe being catty again? I was not going to say anything to Raj. That was the last thing on my mind. Then why did she do this? Does the Universe have something against me?

Is it because I lied to Mum and Dad about Samar? Is this the Universe getting back at me for that? Because I thought we covered that when Mum and Dad refused to speak to me. And also, Samar was the dick in that one because he had a long-term girlfriend, so really, if anything, he should be the one getting punished, not me.

The workings of the Universe continue to confound me. I no longer believe that she means well. I do believe she has a slightly twisted sense of humour. I suspect she is just a categorical bitch and occasionally lets things slide, which is when we're truly happy. Have you noticed how few periods of our lives are ever genuinely happy with nothing stressful hanging in the background? That's the Universe controlling our lives.

'Is there anything I can do to make you feel better?' Sanjay says when I continue to look morosely into the distance.

I lean back in my chair and look at him with a smile. 'Have you ever been a fuckboy?'

Sanjay raises his eyebrows and then freezes. 'Yes', he says, looking rather embarrassed. 'At uni.'

'Really? Why don't I know about this?' I lean forward.

'It was a girl on my course. I knew she fancied me but I didn't fancy her.'

'Don't be short on the detail, Sanj. What happened?'

Sanjay sighs as if telling me his fuckboy tale would lead me to sever ties with him. 'It was at a club night. We got drunk and I was... horny.'

'Of course,' I nod understandingly.

'And she was... there. Basically, we kissed and she told me she liked me. I said I liked her too, she agreed to go home with me, and then I told her that I couldn't date her.'

'Nice one', I say after a pause. 'Truly.'

'I know, but I've changed.'

I nod. 'I'm sure you have.'

'Have you ever been a fuckgirl? Is that a thing? Do girls fuck around?'

'Sure we do.' I giggle. 'Since David I've only ever fucked around. Well, except for Raj. Apparently, my feelings were too deep for him so I had to tell him.'

'Were they, actually?'

'No.' I shake my head. 'No, they weren't deep feelings. But it was the first time I felt anything since David and I thought it might be worth exploring, you know?'

Sanjay nods.

'But', I continue, 'if I could tell Raj I fancy him, maybe I'm getting over the David issues?'

'Maybe', Sanjay says. 'It's about time!'

I smile at him. The waiter brings us our doner kebabs and we dig in, and I give him the lowdown on my best fuckboy stories to make him feel a bit better about his appalling past behaviour. That's what friendship is, right?

This Ain't Over Yet

Right after the Christmas party, the office is deadly quiet. I go in for a few days, but seeing as everybody else has taken off for their home countries, I decide to exercise the flexibility option in my work contract and work from home for a bit until the New Year.

I pack up and take off to Abu Dhabi. I want the comfort of home and family life. Things with my parents are almost back to normal. I want the liveliness of my mother being around, of life having a routine. I want a hug from my father, because his hug has the power to fix everything. Well, maybe it can't fix my dignity or the fact that I was so embarrassed I wanted to be swallowed whole by Mother Earth, but it could lend me some comfort.

Staying in Dubai is too painful. Thinking about my drunken confession makes me cringe so hard I feel like I'm going to morph out of my own body to escape. Bit dramatic, I know, but have you ever told someone you fancied them and they said, 'Oh. Yeah, no thanks'? It's awful. So I go to Abu Dhabi and Mum and Dad are overjoyed that everyone will be home for the holidays.

Sounds sweet, doesn't it?

Yeah, well, by New Year's Day, things have taken a turn. The 1st of January. A new beginning for everyone. In my opinion, the most overrated holiday of the year.

Every big holiday is overrated and New Year's is possibly the worst. It's the same jazz every year. Massive plans about two weeks in advance as to how to welcome the new year. I get the fuss, I understand it, but I don't support it. Why do we associate the new year with new beginnings? Unless we're changing, or our circumstances are changing, the New Year isn't going to make anything happen.

But then we come up with New Year's resolutions, don't we? New Year's resolutions are just a magnified version of fixing yourself in the next week. When we eat poorly and drink loads during the weekend, we resolve to fix ourselves on Monday. And when we let things go tits-up for the whole year, we resolve to fix our shit in the new year.

I stopped coming up with any New Year's resolutions a few years ago because I realised that if I can't be arsed to make any changes in my life to achieve my goals during the year, no amount of 1st January blessings is going to make me do it.

I wish I could say the same about my parents. As we sit together for lunch on New Year's Day, I get a growing sense of what their New Year's resolution might be.

My instinct, of course, is correct. Their New Year's resolution apparently is to find me a husband. For fuck's sake.

'So, what have you thought about your future?' Mum says.

The only thing I have thought about so far in the New Year is how I desperately want to go back to Dubai and go to the office. Working from home in Abu Dhabi is proving to be quite suffocating. I feel like I have more information about the gossip in my mother's circle than I would like to know. I know that Dolly Aunty's sister-in-law gifted a 15 AED perfume to

Lovely Aunty on her birthday. I know that Pinky Aunty is doing a housewarming party and not inviting Dolly Aunty because she's a cheapskate and hence an unacceptable addition to the party. I'd have no idea about any of this if I was still in Dubai. But I fear that my desire to go back to Dubai is not what Mum's after. I also briefly think about joking with Sanjay about my New Year's resolution to quit smoking, but again, not what she's after.

'Umm', I start. I have nowhere to go with this sentence. I shrug and stay quiet.

'So, Samar is in the past', Dad says. 'Maybe it's time you thought about pursuing someone else.'

Like Raj? Shut up, Sassy.

I groan. 'This again?'

'Yes, start the year afresh. New year, new man.' Dad chuckles.

'We have to think about this', Mum says.

'Why? Why do we *have* to?'

'What, so you won't get married then?' Dad says.

'I will, but not just yet. Dad, seriously, can we not do this, please? I feel like I'm listening to a broken record.'

'*Beta,* why don't you understand? If you start looking now, you think you'll get married right away?' Dad snaps. 'These things take months, even years.'

'See, you'll meet someone', Mum says. 'You won't like the first person you meet. You'll meet a few of them. You'll date them for a few months at least. You'll get engaged, that's another year. By the time you meet someone tolerable you'll be twenty-six. That is a good age to be married.'

'But Mum, I'm not ready!'

Mum sighs and looks at Dad as if to say *I don't know how to knock sense into this girl.*

I sigh as well. 'Okay, how about this?' I start. 'We don't talk about it until at least my twenty-fifth birthday. I'm not ready right now, but a few months from now, we can check in again and we can... talk about this.'

Mum and Dad look at each other again.

'Okay', Dad says. 'Twenty-five.'

I text Trisha to tell her the latest development.

Trisha: Loool I did the same thing! I asked to wait until 25 too.
Alia: Well, only 6 months to go.

Peer Pressure

It almost feels like I'm waiting for my prison sentence, waiting for my twenty-fifth birthday. But life has really gone by in a blur.

All of January was spent catching up with work after the hiatus that the world took during Christmas. The new year was suddenly about new processes and new frameworks, so work was properly busy. It was lucky, though, because I didn't have to focus any energy on not being awkward around Raj, who was still in the UK. He came into my life like a gust of wind and now he was gone, having left nothing but sand in my eyes.

February is a short month anyway, but even Valentine's Day came up too fast. How were we just celebrating the beginning of the new year, and now we're already on to celebrating Cupid?

And then March sticks its ugly rear in our faces. I have never cared for March. It's the end of the financial year so work gets extra stressful, but it's also the time that it starts to get hot again in Dubai. March is like a constant reminder of reality: hot and stressful.

This time, March comes with an announcement in the form of Meher showing up with a man for weekend drinks with me and Sanjay.

'Guys, this is Akash', she says with a shy smile.

He smiles at us. 'Nice to meet you guys.'

It all makes sense now. The reason Meher hasn't been showing up to our shenanigans regularly is this man right here. It's always a man, isn't it? Any time a woman loses interest in the bulk of her social life, it's because of a man. It's sad but true. We all say we won't be the type of person who forgets about her friends when she gets a boyfriend, but we end up prioritising the boyfriend. We aren't kids, though, and if someone needs to take a step back from social commitments to focus on a relationship, it's not the end of the world.

I smile back at Akash. 'Nice to meet you too.'

'Nice to have some guy energy around here', Sanjay says with a chuckle, shaking his hand.

Akash sits down next to Meher. He is quite tall and especially so next to Meher, who is small and petite. He has on glasses and looks a little bit nervous. It's understandable; she's probably told him all sorts of stories about how amazing we are.

We learn that Akash is originally from Hounslow in London and moved to Dubai a few years ago after med school in Nottingham. I joke about how every Punjabi knows someone who lives in Hounslow. He doesn't laugh.

We learn that Akash found Meher on Facebook through mutual friends and tried his luck by DM-ing her. Luckily Meher responded, but only to say she didn't know him. He followed up with an apology and a sincere attempt to say he just wanted to get to know her. To an outsider it sounded like the ultimate sliding-into-your-DMs story, but Meher was happy and Akash doesn't seem like a serial killer or rapist, so we are happy for her.

Akash and Meher have been dating for the past four months and their parents are delighted. I can imagine Meher's mother being over the moon, and I can also imagine her telling my mother all about it, seeing as our mothers are friends too. I make a mental note to tell Meher to try and keep this from my mother. I don't need another reason for my mother to think of Meher as the daughter she would rather have.

'Oh, I think Mum was on the phone to her this afternoon actually', Meher says apologetically after Akash leaves to go to another party.

I sigh. 'Never mind. It was bound to happen. I'm happy for you, though', I add with a smile. 'How are things going with him anyway?'

'Really good.' She nods with a shy smile.

'Yeah?'

'Yes absolutely. There's no games with him. He tried to pull the casual card with me, and I said no, and well, things have been great since then.'

'What do you mean?'

'Well, he said that he wanted to keep things casual and see where we go', Meher says. 'But I said I don't want any of that casual crap because I know what that really means.'

Sanjay is listening more keenly now. 'What does it really mean?'

'It means that he's laying the groundwork for a breakup where I can't make him feel bad about it', Meher says, rolling her eyes. 'If we break up, I can't get emotional because we agreed things were casual between us.'

I look at Sanjay, who is smiling knowingly.

'That you don't have a snarky comeback to this tells me Meher is right', I say pointedly.

He shrugs with a grin.

'So, anyway', Meher continues, 'I said I didn't want that. If we're in this, we're in it for the long haul.'

Sanjay looks up. 'Wow, and he stayed?'

'Yeah, I guess he was kind of into me', Meher says cautiously.

I raise my eyebrows. This is literally the most straightforward romance story I have ever heard. No ups and downs. Just ups. So it is possible to have a relationship where you come clean about what you want and what you expect. It is possible to do that from the off. What sort of world is that?

Later, I mention this to Trisha and she laughs at me, as usual.

'Yeah, it is possible', she says. 'That's how Balveer and I happened. I think you'll find that most of the time it's the relationships with the least amount of drama that last.'

'Really?'

'Yeah. Why do you think none of my exes lasted? We were too chaotically dramatic for anything to work.'

'Huh. Good for Meher, then.'

'Mum told me Meher is seeing someone', Trisha adds with a grin.

I roll my eyes. 'Of course she did.'

'She's hoping that it will put some peer pressure on you.'

'I thought that might happen.'

She grins. 'Is it working?'

'Decidedly not.'

'What do you have against dating?'

'I have nothing against dating or marriage.' I shake my head. 'I just wish we could look more favourably upon alternate lifestyles where I end up in a long-term relationship with a Golden Retriever. I think that would be quite fulfilling.'

A pregnant pause.

'Please don't say that in front of Mum and Dad.'

IndianRishtaa.com

In keeping with Trisha's advice, I don't bring up the alternate lifestyle where I live with a dog. There is no point.

I turn twenty-five in enough splendour to make me forget that Mum and Dad have every intention of fixing me up the very next day. Sanjay and Meher organise a lovely pool brunch for me in the popular JBR district in Dubai. Amidst the freely flowing prosecco, fried appetisers, decadent desserts, cooling off in the pool, and shimmying with Brazilian dancers, I don't think about getting married at all. I think about how I want the topless male dancers to make a big deal about my birthday and pay me special attention.

The next day brings a completely different set of emotions and a different celebration. Family brunches are always much more sophisticated and much less exhausting than a regular Dubai brunch. And my family do give me thoughtful presents every year. Except this year, Mum and Dad have given me an additional present I never asked for.

They have created my profile on IndianRishtaa.com.

In the dating game, there are several ways you can meet your "person." Here is what it looks like, in decreasing order of acceptability:

Organically (e.g., in a coffee shop, pub, bookstore, etc.)

On a dating app

On a hookup app

On a matrimonial app

My parents have literally gone and put me on the lowest order of the dating spectrum.

No offense to people who do meet on matrimonial apps, but I feel it's a bit insulting when your parents have to take control of your love life and basically leave you out of it, like you can't be trusted with your own life decisions. It's not alien to Indian culture, but I find it insulting, nonetheless. In effect, my parents have decided to insult me on my birthday.

'Are you being serious?' I say to them when they happily make the announcement.

'Yes', Mum says. 'It's high time now, you're twenty-five.'

'Yes, yes, I know', I snap. 'But why IndianRishtaa.com? I thought you had someone in mind? I thought that was why you were on my case?'

'No, we don't know anyone, *that's* why we want you to get serious.'

Fucking helllll. Alia. Why? Alia. Stop this.

I sigh.

I don't know what to feel. I've been on dating apps before and they've been quite horrific experiences, I won't lie. This is not going to be an online dating app kind of experience, but it is going to be horrific in other ways. Trisha was on it in her prime, and I don't think she ever truly recovered. This isn't even an app for the bride and the groom. It's an app for the parents of the bride and the groom. If I match with someone on this app, the notification goes through to my phone and the groom's phone and also to the parents' phones. It's like an adult version of a parent-teacher conference where the parents are going to sit with the teacher, i.e., IndianRishtaa.com creators, and ask them how their kids are performing. How is this not horrific?

I want to throw up a little bit.

I am confused. Does this mean I am now going to be going out with men who have already received an approval rating from my parents? Can I trust their rating? I know they want what's best for me, but they also thought Samar might be the one. That little tryst with destiny only proved to me that the one person whose judgement I can trust blindly is me.

How have I ended up at the bottom of the barrel? Most people on these apps have either been too shy their entire lives to date anyone or have just been through a terrible breakup and their parents have decided to take control because clearly they cannot be trusted to make important decisions on their own. Either way, whichever category you fall in, you are a little bit sad. That I have ended up on the same app is very telling about my own life. I haven't been too shy to date. In my prime, Sassy Alia has actually been in awe. It is only after moving to Dubai and starting a new job, and of course my David Preston issues, that I slowed down with the sassy life and focussed more on the professional life.

I also feel like my life is now over. My parents have decided that I have lived my own life long enough; it's time to get me married. When I tell them this, they chide me.

'Why do you feel marriage is the end of the world? Trisha is married and she's clearly thriving', Mum argues. 'Why do you think you won't have that?'

'Because!' I start. 'You make marriage sound like... a task. "You have to get married by twenty-five. You have to have kids by thirty".'

'There's nothing wrong in getting your life sorted at the right time.'

'Yes, yes, I know', I snap, 'but there's no excitement there. Looking for someone on this app is so... clinical. There's nothing enjoyable about this process.'

My mother stares at me. 'You can enjoy after you're married.'

I find this amusing. Anything you want to do as an Indian woman, you can do after you're married. Mum, I want to get my hair dyed. *Do it after you're married, whatever colour your husband likes.* Mum, I want to get a tattoo. *Do it after you're married.* Mum, you never let me stay out. Why do I have to come back by midnight? *You live in our house, so you follow our rules. When you live in your husband's house, you can stay out as late as he likes.*

I look at my parents' faces. Hopeful faces. I sigh. I could get on the app to make them happy. Keep the peace in the house. But I won't marry any of them.

'Alright, I guess we're doing this.'

I am officially at the bottom of the barrel. Happy twenty-fifth, Alia.

Not surprisingly, my parents have already created my profile and have just been waiting for my approval to go live.

ALIA ARORA, Dubai

(A picture of me from Trisha's wedding, wearing a sari)
Date of Birth: 27th June 1993
Star Sign: Cancer
Kundli: N/A
Place of Birth: Abu Dhabi
Grew up in: Abu Dhabi
Religion: Sikh
Education: BA and MSc - King's College London
Profession: Other (Researcher is not considered a conventional job amongst Indian families and so didn't even show up as an option)
Complexion: Fair
Height: 165 cm
Body Type: Athletic ('Alia, please stop lifting weights, you should be slender! Look at your chest, there's nothing there.' 'Mum!')
Income: disclosed to Premium Members
Drinking: No ('What!?' I say in disbelief. 'Some families don't like it.' 'Yes, but I do!')
Smoking: No ('What!?' I say inwardly because smoking is a no-no amongst my people)
Food habits: Non-vegetarian

Bio:
I am a friendly person and have been raised with great values ('what are "great" values? That doesn't mean anything'). *I have been taught to respect elders, and I am attached to my sister as well. I love reading, cooking* ('I fucking don't.' 'Alia, language!'),

socializing, and enjoy watching detective shows ('Well, at least that's true').

I am looking for an individual who is well educated, financially stable, understanding, and open-minded. He should be a non-smoker ('Are these my preferences or yours?'). *We should both be able to establish a level of mutual understanding for each other's professional lives. He should also have a good sense of humour.*

If you would like to connect with me, please contact Mr. N. Arora (+971xxxxxxxx5)

Full contact details visible with Premium membership

'Well, I mean, this is a load of bollocks', I say, 'but I don't know what else to say so... fine. Hit Send.'

'Alia, you don't have to be so disrespectful, you know', Mum says. 'Calling it bollocks. You think we like spending hours on the internet looking for a husband for you?'

'I don't think you like it, and I know I don't like it. That's why I fail to understand what the rush is', I say. 'Yes, I know everything has a timeline, but life can't be planned like that. If I'm not interested right now, that's it, I'm just not interested.'

Mum rolls her eyes. 'So sorry, Alia. So sorry that we are spending all this time and money looking for a nice husband for you. If you marry someone who earns well, has a solid educational background, has a loving family, you will be doing us a favour, no?'

And just like that, another wedge is inserted into our relationship. Yippee.

Diljit Dosanjh[10]

Things with Raj get back to normal, but normal prior to the kiss had included regular flirtation. Given that kissing is now off limits, flirtation takes a back seat, and what we are left with is conversation. So things aren't 'normal' per se but as normal as I can hope them to be.

Luckily the search for a husband on IndianRishtaa.com doesn't kick off quite the way my parents hoped. They had hoped to be bombarded by messages and phone calls from keenos—which they have been—but the keenos haven't been entirely desirable. If my parents are ruling them out, I am glad. What I am not glad about is my parents stressing out about what they see as a lack of decent boys.

'There is literally nobody here', Mum says one day. 'They either look strange, or they don't earn enough money. What *are* we going to do?'

They could deactivate the account.

So in the midst of the awkwardness with Raj and my parents stressing out, I can't seem to find the joy in the summer.

10   Popular Punjabi singer with a large female fan base, known for his vocal range and sense of style

And then one day my parents find theirs when they are alerted to the existence of one Puneet Singh, a doctor from Chandigarh, India.

I am not entirely sure why, but members of the medical professional community seem to be every Indian parent's wet dream. A guy could be the biggest dickhead known to mankind, a serial killer, the biggest racist in the world, but if he's a doctor, anything is excused.

So when Mum sees that a doctor is interested in my profile, she comes quite close to losing it.

'Alia, look, he's quite good looking too!' she said, her eyes lighting up as we sit together in the living room, me trying to watch telly and Mum swiping like a pro.

I turn to look at her and lean in cautiously to see what she describes as "quite good looking".

Well, I'll be damned. He actually is quite good looking. Well done, Mum.

I reach my hand out for her phone. Mum really has done well. He is a Sikh man so he wears a turban, and quite proudly too. He seems tall and muscular with broad shoulders and a warm smile. His eyes are a light shade of brown, and in each of the pictures he wears a different coloured turban that matches his outfits. Quite a good dresser indeed. He gives off distinctly Diljit Dosanjh vibes in his appearance, except with a softer face. For the first time in a long time, I am intrigued by a proposition Mum is making.

'What do you think?' she said, watching my face carefully.

I nod. 'He's quite good looking, yes.'

'He is! Twenty-nine, doctor, lives in Dubai! You can easily date him!'

'Alright, Mum, calm down. Let me at least chat to the guy first', I say, standing up to get a glass of water and also escape the sudden excitement in the room.

But I am interested. A good-looking prospect? I can live with that. I could thrive on that.

Mum shows the profile and photos of Dr. Puneet Singh to Dad, who looks at my face carefully.

I shrug and say, 'Yeah, I can chat to him, you can give him my number.'

'Much better looking than Samar', Dad says, handing the phone back to Mum and turning back to his iPad to continue watching golf tutorials.

The summer has taken an unexpectedly pleasant turn for Mum and Dad. For me? Well, I'm not sure yet.

Puneet: Hello. Puneet this side, your father gave me your number.

How formal. Puneet this side. This side of what? Oh, Sassy, are you going to be nit-picky? *Yes, I'm always going to be the bitch that you claim you are not.*

Alia: Hi Puneet, how's it going?
Puneet: Good ji, you tell? Kidhan[11]?

Wait, what? He's one of those? He's a Samar in doctor disguise?

---

11 'How are you?' in Punjabi

I frown.

Alia: Good, thanks.

I continue frowning and set my phone down with a drowning sensation in my stomach. Part of me feels like it dies when I get a text like this. IndianRishtaas are literally juicing the life out of me. It is evident that I will have superficial issues with his grammar and the way he speaks, and Mum and Dad will tell me off for being unreasonable and judgmental.

Punjeet: So, this is little bit new to me! Is this your first time on IndianRishtaa?

I facepalm at his grammar, aware that those sitting around my desk are starting to wonder what is happening to me.

Alia: Yes, my first time as well.
Puneet: So what do you do?
Alia: I work in research for a business publication. And you're a doctor?
Puneet: Haanji[12]!
Alia: What kind of doctor?
Puneet: Ortho. If you want free orthotics, I can give you haha
Alia: Aren't they quite expensive? Are you actually authorised to provide them to patients free of charge?
Puneet: No yaa I'm just joking.

12 'Yes'

Alia, what the fuck does 'no yaa' mean? Also, good one on quashing the flirtation already. Very sassy move.

Puneet: So Alia tell me, you wanna meet? Maybe it's easier.

I sigh. I could potentially not meet him, drag out this conversation, then ghost him. But that would lead to loads of questions from Mum and Dad. Besides, maybe he just texts weird. Maybe he's better at in-person conversation.

Alia: Sure. Whereabouts do you live?
Puneet: I live in JLT yaa

Seriously, what the fuck is 'yaa'?

Alia: Do you drive?
Puneet: No yaa I just came from Chandigarh. License is on my list.
Alia: Okay, maybe we can meet in one of the JLT clusters. Thursday suit you?
Puneet: Done done Alia ji.

Fucking hell, I don't think I can match this energy.

I heave a heavy sigh.

'Alright', Aisling pipes in. 'What's going on? You seem stressed.'

I turn to look at her. *Hmm. White lady. Could she understand our problem? Probably not, but she could express how outrageous this is and we could form a community.*

'So, my parents', I say. 'Well, they're quite keen on me getting married quite quickly.'

'Aren't you like… twelve?' Aisling says with an incredulous smile.

I grin. 'In my head, yes,'

I recite the tale of the last seven months to Aisling and as predicted, she seems quite confused as to how things work in the Indian community. I tell her about how Mum and Dad tried to set me up with Samar and how I went out with him a few times despite positively hating him. I tell her about how Samar got engaged a few days after our "breakup" and how Mum and Dad tried to get me to move on to the next man and how I had managed to keep them off my case until I turned twenty-five and how the man I am now chatting to at age twenty-five texts like he is fresh off the boat from India.

'Is that a problem for you? Like, could you date someone from India?'

I shrug. 'I don't know.'

'Wait, so who do you normally date?'

I smile awkwardly and take her through the very brief history of my dating life that started with David Preston, took an unexpected turn into flings, and culminated with deep and meaningful relationships with such men as Italian Man, Man from Liverpool St. Station, Man from Starbucks outside Holborn Station, and Man from the Chemistry department.

'And were all these men white?' Aisling's clearly enjoying herself.

'Man from Liverpool St. Station was Lebanese British', I say after a pause. 'But I don't even think Indian is the problem! The problem is people like Samar who chat shit.'

'So, let's say... let's say someone like Raj! He's Indian, isn't he?'

I raise my eyebrows.

A pause later, 'Yes, he is.'

'And he's a Sikh too!'

'Yes, I know.'

'Oh, my God, Alia, your husband has been waiting for you at the office and you've been making your parents go through apps!'

I shake my head vigorously. 'Raj is not going to be my husband. He's a colleague.'

'Yalla! Get on the dating wagon, then! Get on an app or something that kids these days are on.'

'That's not the point! The point is that I don't want to be with anybody right now! I'm happy the way I am.'

'Oh. Well that's a tricky situation.'

Indeed.

White People's FAQs about Indian Matrimony

Q. So do you have to marry an Indian man then?

Yes

Q. What if you were to fall in love with a white man?

I mean, I'm not necessarily attracted to white men all that much, in terms of thinking of them with a long-term perspective. When I see white men, I don't even think of them that way, so it's sort of been wired into my system that I am not to look at a white man that way. Obviously, for shenanigans, ethnicity is not important.

Q. But what if you had a white colleague and you really hit it off and you just fell madly in love with each other? What then?

Then I would be paving the way for a lot of family drama. My parents can be persuaded but it won't be pleasant, and frankly, the amount of effort alone makes me not want to ever think of a white man that way. For shenanigan purposes I'd be happy with a white man but never for something serious.

Q. So you'd have to marry a Hindu man then?

No, I'm Sikh. The preference would be Sikh.

Q. What's the difference between Hindu and Sikh? Aren't they the same?

They're as same as Christianity and Judaism are the same.

Q. So you can't marry a Hindu?

I can, but it would be their second preference.

Q. Can you choose your own husband? Like, can you date someone and introduce them to your parents?

Yes.

Q. Then why don't you just find someone?

Because I don't want a husband right now; doesn't matter where he comes from, me or my parents.

Q. What happens if you don't marry?

Family arguments, drama, yelling.

Q. I find it so strange that you have to go through this!

Yes. Was there a question?

The Doctor Will See You Now

Friday evening should be a fun time, not a time for me to be battling nausea from anxiety about going out on a date. A date shouldn't be making me anxious at all. Yet, here I am, all dressed up for a date but not feeling particularly keen. My clothes say "let's do this" but my face says "y tho".

I head out from work toward the southern end of the city, which I know is going to be bursting with traffic. I make it into a cosy little coffee shop in the JLT district and choose a sofa that doesn't exude romance. The cosiness of the cafe is disturbing enough as it is. I don't want any additional romantic fanfare.

We had decided on six o' clock. It is now five minutes past six and there is no sign of Puneet. I remember Samar's words: 'Indians aren't punctual'. If we aren't punctual people, am I to spend most of my life waiting for things to happen? It doesn't seem like a very good use of our very limited time on this earth.

At ten minutes past six I see the tall figure of Puneet enter the cafe. He has on a red turban, red *kurta,* blue jeans on long legs, and Aviator glasses that he takes off to reveal his beautiful face. I can almost hear the song "Gulabi Pagg" by Diljit Dosanjh playing in the background as he walks toward me with a broad smile. He truly is a good-looking man. I am in two minds: one governed by Sensible Alia, the other by Nether Alia. I am curious to see which one wins.

'Alia!' he says with a broad smile and a wave. He walks up to where I am seated and shakes my hand. 'Good to meet you finally!' he says with the strongest Punjabi accent I have ever heard in my life.

That's not such a big problem though, is it?

'Yeah, you too', I say with a smile, trying to look friendly and non-judgemental.

He sits down and orders our coffees. We talk about our day. He tells me about his life as an orthopaedic surgeon and I tell him about my life as a researcher. He likes to spend his weekends chilling with his cousins at movie or game nights. Work can be quite stressful for a doctor, so when the chance arises he likes to take a step back and have a laid-back weekend. I feel silly now admitting that my idea of a nice weekend is going to a pool brunch and then spending Sunday nursing a hangover. I try to redeem myself by letting him know some of my other interests, like my love for Dubai Opera and how some of the shows really are quite exquisite. He nods and says that he never truly understood opera.

I can't help but notice how different we seem. He seems like a super mature person, spending his weekends in a super mature way, actually trying to rejuvenate himself. I feel like a child who hasn't quite got over university. If this hadn't been a rishtaa situation, the first thing I might have done would have been to snigger at his accent with Trisha, because that's the sort of person I am. I am a child, mocking someone for something so trivial instead of appreciating them for their accomplishments.

'What are you up to this weekend then?' I say, aware that I might be running out of things to say to this man.

'Mom *da* birthday *si kal*', he says, unexpectedly switching to Punjabi to tell me that it's his mum's birthday tomorrow. 'So, flying to Delhi tomorrow to see her.'

'Oh, that's nice of you!'

He nods, continuing to smile nervously. For both our sakes, I wonder if we can end this now.

'And who else is in your family?' he asks.

'I've got an older sister.'

'She's married?'

'Yes.'

'She has kids?' he asks after a pause.

I want to laugh at how ridiculous it is that we've run out of topics to talk about so quickly that Trisha's children is what we're on now.

'No, she doesn't', I say.

He nods.

'And how many kids you think you want?'

I raise my eyebrows.

'Ideally, I want a dog', I say.

He laughs. 'No, seriously, how many?'

'I haven't really thought about it, if I'm honest. Maybe one, or maybe really just a dog.'

'Oh', he says with another nod. 'Hmm', he says. 'Alia, let's get the bill?'

I nod at this rather abrupt end to our date as he signals to the waiter for the bill.

With another awkward smile, we part ways.

Was this the best date of my life? No, I don't think so.

An hour later my phone buzzes to a text and I cannot help but smile.

Puneet: Hello Alia ji
It was really very nice meeting you
But I don't think it will click with us
Good luck for your search

I like this one. Had the balls to immediately say no. Very nicely done.

Another hour later, my phone buzzes again. This time, a call from my father.

'Hmm', he starts. 'What happened? How was it with Puneet?'

'Uh, he actually sent me a text to end things.'

'Why?'

'He said it doesn't seem like we'll click... so, that's over.'

'Hmm, okay. His father sent me a text too.'

'Oh? What did he say?'

'He said you're outspoken. They're looking for someone humble for their son.'

I pause, outraged. 'His father doesn't even know me! What gives him the right to make comments about me?'

'Whatever it is, I don't know what conversation you had with him, but we'll speak tomorrow, I'm getting another call.'

With that, he hangs up. My outspoken ass wants to have a lie-down and a bottle of wine for dinner.

The Marriage Market

IndianRishtaa.com has been a thoroughly mortifying experience so far, but it is also very amusing to see what the marriage market has to offer. Nothing worth spending time on, because this post isn't about me getting engaged, rather a rant about what I've found in the market so far.

The number of people named Gary Sandhu[13] is ridiculous. If you're going to catfish people, at least make it less obvious.

The number of men with turbans bigger than their own heads is ridiculous too.

The number of men in the "travel industry" is baffling.

Puneet was just one experience. There have been several others.

There was the man who didn't seem to understand the concept of IndianRishtaa.com. In a very unexpected turn of events, he wasn't interested in marriage at all, which should have worked out fine for me because we could have just stopped chatting. But he went ahead and asked for nudes. So that was a no.

Then there was the man who met me for a coffee and asked me what I thought about marriage, which I found to be quite

13   Popular Punjabi singer

a strange question. Would you ever meet a new friend and ask them what they thought friendship was? Or would you ever go out on a date with someone and ask them what they thought a relationship should be like? Actually, yes. But would you do that on the first date? It felt much more like a job interview: 'And what would your ideal role look like?'

I shrugged and tried to dodge the question, but I didn't need to because he spent the next twenty minutes describing what he thought marriage should be like. He also proceeded to chide me for not having any thoughts about it, and I proceeded to tell him that his application to marry me had been declined and that I would not be saving his CV on file for future job openings.

Then there was the doctor from the UK that my parents insisted I speak to only because he was a doctor and he was from the UK.

'We thought you liked the UK?' Mum said.

'Yes, I did, when I lived there, but now I'm happy where I am', I said. 'And this man's face looks like a pillow!'

'Alia, you don't look like Ms. India', my mother snaps, always my biggest cheerleader. 'Don't be so judgemental.'

'Mother, I don't think I look like Ms. India either, but please look at his face and tell me this is the best you think I can do.'

I wasn't even joking. He genuinely looked like a pillow. He wore a white turban in his photo and a white shirt. His face was big and round and white, as was his white turban, and he had practically no neck. If there was ever a time to be superficial about looks, this was it. I know that in the future, the chances of my husband becoming a round Uncle are quite high, but I would rather I didn't start with him when he was already at that stage of his life.

Then there was the banker who very proudly claimed that he had anger issues and was in therapy to bring it under control. Lovely.

There have been several other catfish accounts on the website. They follow the same pattern. A super good-looking guy in the pictures. UK education, and always top tier, so think Cambridge and Oxford. Always a doctor, because they know what's going to attract the ladies. Always a salary well over GBP 100k a year. Always a US contact number with the United Nations listed as the employer. It is uncanny how each of these has basically the same credentials. How do I know it's a catfish situation? Because the person on the other end of the messaging chain can't keep up with his lies. The profile I was contacting had Cambridge listed under education, and when I asked him more questions about it, he couldn't even name the college he'd been at. This is preliminary investigative work. Let's say someone doesn't delve too deep into your educational background and agrees to meet you. What then? What happens when they meet you and realise you look nothing like your pictures?

The latest is Harjit Dhaliwal. Works as a consultant at one of the Big 4, studied in Germany and worked in London for a while. Recently moved to Dubai. Mum and Dad are overjoyed. Me, on the other hand, just a little bit sceptical. But hey, I'm open to being proven wrong.

Highly Qualified Moron

Today is the day. Mum and Dad have not been able to stop gushing about Harjit Dhaliwal. In their minds, a man with a comfortable salary and family values close to ours is the perfect fit. If he ticks those two boxes, everything else can be ignored. They know that his salary already ticks the box, so the next big thing is family values, for which I will be the assessor.

'He is highly, highly qualified', Dad keeps reminding me.

'Really, Alia, I don't think you'll find a better match', Mum says.

I see what they mean. In terms of qualifications, he really is something else. Two bachelor's degrees in the Sciences and an MBA. This man truly must be intelligent. Or else it begs the question as to why he needed two degrees in the first place. Also, these are his educational qualifications and I am not entirely sure how that is going to ensure he is the best carnal and matrimonial match for me.

Still, I play along. I ask for his photos, which prove underwhelming. The man wears a grey turban, beige trousers, and greige shirt. Really, could he have thought of a combination duller than that? To top that, his beard and moustache are untidy. I'm not anticipating huge sparks of desire.

Trisha advises me to play along.

'Honestly, he seems like a thirty-two-year-old virgin', she says matter-of-factly. 'Just be confident and intelligent and it's going to scare him away. Just be you.'

I arrive at the little cafe on Emaar Boulevard and within minutes, so does Harjit. I have to give it to him: He is already winning in the tardiness category.

He smiles awkwardly and shakes my hand and sits diagonally from me. I don't understand his decision, but I don't question it either. He stays silent for a few seconds, so I cut the silence.

'What would you like to drink?'

He sighs. 'Um... chocolate milkshake?'

'Okay.' Unusual choice, but I respect that.

I signal the waiter to take our orders. He leaves and we are left to make conversation, which at this moment, seems like the most complicated ask.

I smile at Harjit. He smiles and looks away.

What? Sassy Alia laughs in my head.

'So, what do you do?' I say.

'I work as a consultant here in Downtown.'

'Oh, right.' A pregnant pause. Then, 'I work as a researcher for a business publication.'

He nods.

'How are you finding Dubai so far?' I say.

He looks around for a second. Then, 'It's good.'

I smile and nod.

Silence.

'I'm sorry, are you quite alright?'

He nods. 'Yes.'

More silence.

'What do you normally do on weekends?' I ask eventually.

'I normally sleep in on weekends. I clean my house. Maybe catch a film on TV.'

This is going to be hard, hard work.

'Right.' I nod. 'Have you seen much of Dubai then? Since you've been here, I mean.'

'Yes', he nods. 'I went to the beach.'

'Oh, which one?'

'Jumeirah Beach.'

'And did you like it?'

'It was alright.'

'How about Downtown? Have you been to any of the attractions? The Burj, the Dubai Mall, perhaps Dubai Opera?'

'No, I don't like any of these things.'

'Right.' I nod.

He looks away from me again.

'Okay, I think this has been a mistake', I finally say. 'You are clearly not happy to be here, you won't even look at me, and you won't even ask me anything. I'm just going to get my coffee to go.'

'Okay', he says slowly with a shrug.

Seriously? That's it? Okay? What the actual fuck.

I ask the waiter to bring the drinks in to-go cups and for the bill. Harjit doesn't offer to pay or even split it. He doesn't even look at the bill.

We get up to leave.

'Well, this has been...' I start and pause.

Go on, what has this been? Great? We should do this again some time?

'...an utter waste of time, I'm sorry', I finish.

Once inside my car, I dial the home number frantically.

'Hello?' Mum answers.

'Mum?'

'Alia, are you okay? Are you crying?!'

'Mum, I need a break', I say with my ugly crying voice, wiping tears from my eyes.

The Most Frustrated of Frustrated Women

I am excruciatingly frustrated. And I am about to unload on my parents.

I am frustrated and emotional because a logical conversation with my parents seems impossible. I am either categorically labelled a drama queen or accused of being too whitewashed to understand Indian societal norms and culture.

Are you telling me that all Indian people everywhere want to get married? That would mean that Indian fuckboys don't exist, and although I have not encountered any so far, I have heard a lot about them. Are they all whitewashed too?

Maybe I have been influenced by other cultures and norms. But can one blame me? Dubai is a tapestry of cultures and ideas. Even if I wasn't in Dubai, the world we live in has enabled the exchange of ideas to take place at the speed of light. Okay, perhaps not at the speed of light, but very fast. One doesn't even need to actively be a part of a multicultural society to facilitate the exchange of ideas. Whether we like it or not, we are already subconsciously a part of a digitally multicultural society. So, no, there's nothing wrong with me. I am my own person and all ideas float everywhere regardless.

I am mentally exhausted. The sheer act of making small talk with daft prospects is exhausting. Is this what life will be? Every text I get with the words "matrimonial purpose" makes me lose any amount of moisture I might have in my nether region. Seeing as this is a text from someone who could likely be involved in procreation with me, I find this outcome to be quite counterproductive.

I am upset. Are my parents just trying to get rid of me? Am I a terrible inconvenience to them? I moved out a while ago, so I cannot possibly be a physical inconvenience. Is having an unwed daughter so painful that they are willing to pimp me out to the first person they find?

And suddenly others' opinion of me is so important to them? An actual parent has said that they are looking for someone less outspoken than me for their son. How am I meant not to take that as an attack on my characteristics, on my personality? How can Mum and Dad be okay with someone talking about me that way?

I am sexually frustrated. I probably won't talk to my parents about that, but I am hella frustrated in this department. I convince myself that meaningless, feeling-less shenanigans like the good old days will do, but I just can't bring myself to that level anymore. Every emotionally exhausting episode leaves me wanting sexual gratification, yet I can't/don't go through with it. It is not a supply problem. No, the supply of meaningless and feeling-less prospects is at a global high. That is one commodity that never faces supply problems. From my end, though, there is an inconsistency in demand and so, as the buyer too, I am frustrated.

Ugh.

Clink

Everybody seems to be on dating apps. There used to be a stigma around it, but it has worn off. Where businesses are increasingly online, why can't aortic transactions be conducted online too? Do I sound excessively romantic when I say aortic transactions?

The solution to my frustration seems simple. How does one arrive at solutions? By studying the symptoms. My symptoms are easily identifiable. Mental exhaustion, emotional frustration, and the need for sexual release. The answer is sex. Not a doubt about it. Sanjay, of course, agrees with me. Meher, not so much. She thinks I need to address my issues more seriously and have open and honest conversations with my parents about how I want to live my life. That is more work than I am prepared to put in, so for now, we're listening to Sanjay.

During my glorious days of super-intimate relationships with Man from Starbucks and the like, my heart wasn't involved. Thank you, David Preston, for fucking that up. But now my heart seems to be stepping out of retirement and is on the lookout for actual human connection. This is turning out to be quite tiresome, because where does one find this human connection? In my heyday, of course, I could find this organically, but now it seems online dating is all the rage, so online dating is what I must embrace.

Of course, online dating isn't the stigmatic phenomenon it once was. Upon inception it filled an entire generation of people with a level of cringe that has since been replaced with a feeling of surrendering, seeing as the alternatives don't seem to be working.

What do I even want, though? If my parents were involved in this discussion, the answer would be a resounding 'marriage, of course!' If I'm dating to marry, I know that an Indian marriage isn't about the couple at all. It's about the entire troop of the family, led by Col. Mother, with Brigadier Father, a smattering of Captain Aunts and Lieutenant Uncles, all watching the husband and wife in the cadets.

So, am I dating to marry? Fuck no. Before I enter this high-pressure system where the entire family is involved, I want to wade into the swimming pool of relationships, one step at a time. If the temperature feels comfortable, I could jump right in at the right depth, but if it isn't, I'll need time.

I obviously can't tell my parents. They'll go off on a tangent about my age and I have that sumbitch memorised already. I don't need parental involvement at this stage. What I need is to take my time and find out for myself what I like and dislike. For someone whose references are limited to David Preston and the string of follow-up flings, I really have no expectations.

So with a heart filled with a combination of stress from the idea of trying something new and excitement for the same thing, i.e., trying something new, I have created an account on Clink. It seems like the least stressful app out there. I have tried dating apps before and some have been quite unduly sexual in their nature in that upon matching with the men, I receive photos of their genitals that I have not expressly asked to view. On the other end of the spectrum is IndianRishtaa.com, and I am not going back there, no matter what. Clink seems to be the perfect middle ground.

Over the weekend I take some time to see what the sea looks like, this sea that has been proclaiming to be housing all these exciting fish. It seems alright so far. It is definitely reflective of the different types of people one finds in Dubai. With every person that I swipe, I discover a new nationality and a new and interesting job. There are chefs, architects, consultants, bankers, business owners. There are Lebanese, Egyptian, Indian, English, Australian, and Canadian men. And then I find Ishaan.

Ishaan seems lovely. He is an American of Indian origin. Grew up in Seattle. Been in Dubai for the past few years. Works for a local media company. Enjoys brunch and all things Dubai. I swipe right. And it's a match.

That first match gives me a sense of validation I didn't think I needed. I send him a message to say hello. He sends one back right away. He asks me what I do, and I ask him the same thing. He tells me about his life story, which seems rife with American references. I tell him about my own story, which I find stale in comparison.

We talk about Dubai things. This is something two people living in Dubai can never not have anything to say about. He seems clever and witty. He asks if I would like to meet him. I tell him I would. We agree to get a drink the following Friday, seeing as it's Ladies Night in my favourite bar. He would like me to have a good night with free-flowing bevvies and food.

Is this what I want? A clever and witty man who wants me to have a good time? Well, whoever said no to that? Is this possible? Have I already matched with someone I like at the first try? Is this what I needed, to get my parents out of the way? Well, I'll have to go out with him first, but it seems delightful so far. I don't know why people hate online dating so much.

Online Dating
for Dummies

I am super nervous. It's not my first online dating experience, of course, but it's my first since being reborn as New Alia with fewer trust issues and more desire for something heartfelt and not purely physical. Before arriving at the bar, I swipe through his photos multiple times just to make sure that stepping into the world of online dating is going to be worth it.

So far, I think it might be. I mean, he's handsome. Even more so than Raj, and I had at one point thought that gorgeousity should be measured against a benchmark where the upper limit is Raj. Ishaan isn't the tallest of men, but he is taller than me and I'm happy with that. He has a dusky complexion and a thick head of hair coupled with a thick, dark beard. This might be an Indian man thing, being obsessed with a thick head of hair and beard. I have not come across a clean-shaven man since I was nineteen.

When he walks in, I feel butterflies in my stomach. He has on blue jeans and a tight black t-shirt that shows off his chest and shoulders. His smile lights up his eyes and makes me a little nervous.

'Hello!' he says and gives me a hug. I smile as I feel the muscles in his back. I felt no muscles with the Indian Rishtaa guys. This is off to a good start.

'Why didn't you get a drink?' he says. 'I told you to get a drink!'

'I wasn't going to drink by myself!' I protest.

We order our drinks and settle into conversation. He tells me more about life in America, road trips with family, hikes in the summer, and fireworks on the Fourth of July. I tell him that after viewing the Burj Khalifa fireworks, everything else seems tame in comparison. He chuckles and then stops for a second.

'What?' I say. 'Did I offend you?'

'No.' He chuckles again. 'Nothing, just… You're beautiful, you know that?'

'Oh.' I smile.

'Yeah, you're really beautiful.'

Relax, we get it. Sassy Alia rolls her eyes inwardly.

'Thank you', I say, shy.

'And you're reacting exactly as I thought you would', he adds with another chuckle, now leaning in slightly toward me.

Obviously, I panic. But Sassy Alia panics even more, which is surprising because during most of her monologues in my head, she acts like a sex-crazed leopard.

I smile, suddenly feeling very aware of the distance between us that seems to be closing. Luckily, the sound of the waiters singing "Happy Birthday" to one of the girls on the table next to us breaks the tension between us. I have never been more grateful.

Saved by the display of sparklers and confetti, things don't heat up for the rest of the night. But we do flirt. A lot. I've missed this. I've missed being able to caress the man's arm without having to think about the consequences. Imagine touching the arm of an IndianRishtaa. The guy who texts me *matrimonial alliance purpose* is hardly someone who would warrant a sentiment of flirtation from me. But this guy, Ishaan, is shaping up to be everything I have ever wanted. This might literally be the end of the search. Why look any further than the guy who is handsome—ridiculously so—witty, intelligent, and financially secure?

We chat about music and how Bollywood songs are his guilty pleasure. We chat about travel, university, and Indian parents. I realise that being American, he is fully American, unlike me. I am neither fully Indian nor am I Emirati. I am nothing. When I tell him that, he caresses my cheek lightly and says, 'You are not nothing. You are Indian *and* Dubaian. You are two things.'

'That's not a thing', I say. 'But thanks.'

As we stand up to leave the bar, he links arms with me. 'We're both drunk, this will help', he says.

I chuckle as we head out. In the queue for a cab I can sense that his arm has now unlinked and is heading in the general direction of my bottom. I am divided in my mind; one part of me is looking forward to where this could go—the choice is between my flat in Downtown and his flat in the Marina. The other part of me is wondering if I'm ready for a carnal interaction.

Of course, we are. I consult with Sassy Alia. *Um, no?* No?! Then why did you make me shave my legs? *It's been so long since we got any, what if it's changed since then? What if we're terrible at it? What if he makes us do something we don't like?*

What if we shouldn't even be here? What if IndianRishtaa is our destiny and by being here we're pissing off the Gods of the Universe? And we're in a public place, for fuck's sake! We could be arrested for how he is holding us right now!

As Ishaan leans in slowly, I smile. And then I kiss him on the cheek, hail the nearest cab, and bid him goodbye.

Sassy Alia
(The Sex-Crazed Leopard)

I have a bone to pick with Sassy Alia. If she were any other friend who constantly tried to muck about and mess with my head, I would tell her off and even stop seeing her if she got too out of hand. But she is me and I am her and although she is getting out of hand, there is no escaping her. She knows everything. Too much. She knows my fears, my anxieties, and my desires and she is not afraid to juggle with them. She is quite good at it.

Sometimes, I imagine Sassy Alia as a person in her own right. She dresses like a Greek goddess and lies on the sofa sipping ouzo. She is perpetually drunk so she talks shit most of the time, but she also speaks the truth because, as the Punjabi song goes: *daaru peeke sach bolda*[14].

But she is ruining my Clink experience. I literally left a super-steamy date without a kiss. There was no need for her to get involved with her Rishtaa talk. I could have handled it. Yes, PDA is a no in Dubai, but we're not surrounded by coppers. We could have got away with it. It was a first kiss, not a face suck-off.

14   Literally translates to 'drunk man speaks the truth'

But no use crying over spilt milk. Thanks to Sassy Alia, damage has occurred and now I will need to partake in—lead, rather—the damage control. Sassy Alia seems to have got piss drunk on her ouzo. She hasn't said a word all morning; perhaps she has finally passed out. It's just as well, really. She's more of a nuisance than help sometimes.

I pick up my phone, determined to set things straight, but unsure how to. As I begin to type, however, Sanjay's words come to mind: 'Never text a guy first. Let him chase you. If he doesn't, move on.'

I start typing.

Alia: Hey, thanks for last night. Lovely to meet you x
You sound like you had tea with him and are now thanking him for the cake. Try again.
Alia: Heyy
Lovely time last night x
Lose the lovely.
Alia: Heyy
Bangin' time last night x
What the fuck, are you mental?
Alia: Heyy, thanks for last night. I had a great time x
Too keen.

I sigh and put my phone down.
About an hour later my phone buzzes.

Ishaan: Hey hun
I was going to kiss you last night. Too far?

I raise my eyebrows with a smile.

No, too keen. No, fuck off, Sassy. This is my time to shine.

I stare at the message, still smiling but unsure what to say. He is typing again.

Ishaan: Now I wanna see you again and get that kiss

Oh, well done, you. See, by not kissing him last night, you kept him wanting more. Really, you should be thanking me. That was not what you were going for and you know it.

Ishaan is still typing. I debate whether to be cheeky or flirty. Or both.

Alia: Bit keen, aren't you? Lol I type and then instantly delete. *Fucking hell, Alia.*

Ishaan: What are you up to?

Just answer the question!

Alia: Morning. Currently under my duvet and not thinking about getting out of it anytime soon x
Ishaan: I could replace the duvet, you know. Keep you warm.

Just to clarify, we're now sexting? Sassy Alia is confused.

Alia: Go on, then

Really? That's how you show you're keen? Go on, then?

Ishaan: I'm not joking. I want you now.

I raise my eyebrows again. This has taken a very sexy turn very quickly. I am almost not even angry with Sassy Alia anymore. She prompts me to send him my location. And I do.

Alia: See you in 30. If you're late, I'm starting on my own
...
Then,

Ishaan: That's hot

Who Texts Whom First?

Clink is a delight. I don't know why I hesitated to join it. This IndianRishtaa nonsense could have been totally avoided if I'd paid heed to Sanjay's advice that I find myself a boyfriend on my own. Good ol' Sanjay. Always looking out for me.

Ishaan is a delight too. One magical afternoon later he attempts to leave my flat but is evidently not too happy about it.

'I'm only leaving because of this stupid birthday dinner for my friend', he says, planting soft kisses on my neck. I tingle all over, but I hide it from him. I am also pleased that he is showing all the signs of being smitten by me.

'You sound like quite the friend', I say with a grin.

Ishaan chuckles and kisses me. 'You are... something.'

I chuckle.

We have had quite the afternoon. Mostly in each other's faces and personal spaces and overstepping all sorts of physical boundaries. But it's been delightful.

'Seriously, what are you doing to me?' he says, holding my hands and wrapping them around his waist.

'Literally nothing', I say. 'You're just a silly man.'

'I have not stopped thinking about you since last night.'

'I have not stopped thinking about you either.'

'I am going to keep thinking about you all evening', he says between kisses.

'Good.' I grin. 'As you should.'

He groans and detaches himself from me. 'I should get going. Fuck', he adds, turning to look at me with a dazed expression. 'Alright. I'll see you later.'

I close the door and heave a deep sigh as I slump down on the sofa with the unparalleled feeling of gratification. Yes, I'm definitely pleased. After a long, arduous journey with dickheads, I seem to have bagged a normal.

He said he would keep thinking about me. His kisses were so gentle and his words were music to my ears. A normal man was going to be thinking about me. Do I even deserve this? I do, don't I? I have had my fair share—more than my fair share, even—of sample pieces and I have now finally bagged a normal. I do deserve this.

What happens next? Do we go out on more dates? We get to know each other more. We spend more magical days together. Could we go on mini breaks together? We could go to that hotel on the Palm Island, the one with the shimmery ceilings that look like disco balls. We could be the couple that has a private moment in a public pool.

Too far.

Yes. Too far. I have let my imagination run wild after just one date. Maybe it's the happy hormones from this afternoon. But surely, if this feeling, if this spark was to stay between us, we could become an item, couldn't we? Could we not?

Thoughts about Ishaan continue into Monday but unfortunately have to be cut short by work. However, I struggle to devote my undivided attention to it. I occasionally smile thinking about him, but I stop when I realise I'm being weird. I catch a glimpse of Raj. I feel nothing. Of course, I feel nothing. It's all about Ishaan now.

You're being fucking pathetic. Why are you not more excited? *Because you're being pathetic!*

I think about texting him. Nothing too out there, maybe just something raunchy enough to let him know I am thinking about him, but not so raunchy that I reek of desperation. But would that still be too keen? Perhaps best not to say anything and let him take the lead. I wish we didn't have to play these games; I could just tell him I'd spent all day thinking about him. But as Sanjay never ceases to remind me, the dating world comes with a rule book, and not following the rules leads to penalties.

I see on social media that he had a fun evening at his friend's birthday dinner. Some stories from the evening pop up on my feed. I wonder if at any point he got drunk enough to think about me as he said he would. Perhaps not; he would have texted me if he had. Still, I'm not too concerned. We did only just have one proper date. I can't be too hung up on him.

The day ends and I head home. The empty room has an unpleasant echo about it, an echo of Ishaan's absence. When will I see him again? When will I hear from him again?

I open his chat and see that he's online. Does Sanjay really know all about dating? Who made him King of the World anyway? He's definitely not my king, so I should be allowed to text whomever I like, whenever I like.

Alia: Hey you x

Sassy Alia rolls her eyes.

Ishaan appears online again. And then offline.

I am immediately engulfed by an internal whirlpool of thoughts. Why did I do that? Why did I text him?

I put my phone away, turning the screen down. An unpleasant drowning sensation takes over my stomach. I might vomit.

My phone buzzes. My heartbeat speeds up.

It's from work.

I put my phone down again and go into the kitchen to cook. I turn up the music so it's loud enough to tune out the sound of my phone. If Ishaan texts, I'll see it later. If anyone else texts, I won't hear it and it won't trigger my nausea.

About twenty minutes later I walk out of the kitchen. I take a look at my phone. No texts.

Well, this is fucking depressing. Maybe you should listen to Sanj more.

Every time my phone buzzes, I feel a lump in my throat, and when I see it isn't from him, my stomach feels worse. I cannot possibly eat what I have just cooked.

I look at his chat again.

Was I being too keen? *Hey you x* is nothing, though, surely?

Was I too keen while he was here? Did I give him access to my private garden too quickly? He wanted access and I gave it to him. Consent was very much forthcoming from both parties. So, how was I the keeno?

Eventually, I fall asleep and wake up to another day of work and another disappointment in the form of five new emails, one new text from work, and no new text from Ishaan.

Maybe he's busy. But that makes no sense. He was so prompt before we met. And it's been a day since I sent him that text. How long does a reply to *hey you x* take?

Have I been ghosted? Is that it?

Fucking hell, I've been ghosted, haven't I?

Is there a way to confirm this? What if he texts me tomorrow?

I've been ghosted, haven't I?

The New Normal

Ishaan is not a delight. He is a dick. Clink is not a delight either. It is a dick house.

Nobody likes to admit they've been played. For two days after my *hey you x* text I keep trying to convince Sassy Alia that Ishaan is probably just busy and that my text probably got buried deep under his pile of unread texts. Come the weekend, though, I see his story online, showing him and his friends partying at a bar in the Marina. So, Ishaan isn't busy. He is just a dick. And as much as I hate to admit it, I have in fact been played.

I can't believe that I live in a world where people like Ishaan get away with ghosting and where people like me have to ask people like Sanjay for advice on how to navigate the dating world. Sanjay hasn't been in a long-term relationship, but he has been successfully dodging emotional bullets in the dating arena, and so now he is my only source of trusted information on what does and what doesn't hurt in the dating world. Ghosting hurts. But apparently one gets used to it.

I used to think I was clever, but having been so easily played by Ishaan and his smooth words, I am determined to own the dating world. I am going to master it. I don't know what mastering it looks like, but I think I'll know when I have achieved it.

I get back on Clink almost immediately. Ishaan has changed his photo, so clearly he's back at it too. I don't quite understand my purpose of swiping. I am no longer looking for a relationship; rather, I seem to be fuelled by the urge to seek vengeance for having been ghosted. Again, not sure what my course of action will be with this, but I think I'll know when I'm on it.

I swipe through profiles, carefully scanning each. This time, anyone with a basic profile is naturally out. I settle on someone called Jag.

Jag, 26
25 km away

Teacher
Indian from Kenya

Lives in Dubai
From Nairobi

I swipe through his photos. Very good looking, well-built, broad shoulders, clean shaven. His photos show his travel escapades in Kenya, other parts of Africa, one atop an elephant, showing off his muscular physique, and a final one from a bar. He seems interesting. Definitely not basic.

Looking for someone to share butter chicken with.

I could go for some butter chicken.
I swipe right. It's a match.

Alia: Hate to say it, but you'll need to conquer the depths of Karama for good butter chicken.

I send the message and sigh. I realise my purpose: to gain my dignity back by not being played this time.

Jag: I thought it might be! How are you, Alia? Btw can I just say, you are beautiful. Love your smile x

One Ishaan ago, I would have blushed at the message. Now, I feel nothing. One Ishaan ago, I could feel.

Alia: Aren't you sweet x

We chat intermittently throughout the day and he tells me about his teacher job. He moved to Dubai a year ago and has been enjoying life out here so far. I tell him about Abu Dhabi and the experience of growing up here. He seems polite and kind. But so was Ishaan. And so was David. I wonder if this will go tits-up too. Sassy Alia assures me that it will. An inner positive voice that lives deep down says, *Don't be like that.*

We continue to chat over the next few days. He tells me about his family in Kenya and the welfare projects he has running back home. He wishes to give back to the community that has given him so much. He really does seem like a nice man and I sense my animosity wavering.

He asks me questions about my life and seems genuinely interested, asking me how the transition was from London back to Abu Dhabi. I tell him it was challenging in a way that not many people understand. I tell him about the person I became in London and how that person now lives in my head rent-free. I choose not to tell him that I call her Sassy Alia and imagine her sipping ouzo and dressed like a Greek goddess because he doesn't need to know the inner workings of my brain just yet.

He sympathises. He tells me he studied in Leicester and had a similar culture shock when he moved back to Kenya. He tells me how he is more Kenyan than he is Indian. I understand. I relate.

The next day he asks if I would like to get a drink over the weekend. I say yes. He says he will let me pick a spot as I'd be the better judge, having lived here for longer. I pick a rooftop bar in Downtown Dubai. I also resolve not to give him access to my private garden immediately after the first date, so as not to prompt Ishaan-like behaviour.

But what if he's lovely? ... We'll think about it.

When Saturday dawns, I realise I'm actually looking forward to this. I'm looking forward to some deep conversations over a glass of wine. He seems like the kind of person who would almost make a date more poetic than romantic, and I want to see what that looks like. Maybe not all men are like Ishaan. No matter what happens though, I am not going to text Jag, or any other guy, first. The *hey you x* has forever tainted my dignity and it sits in my chat staring at me with an evil grin.

Jag and I decide to meet at five o'clock on Saturday so as to get a proper look at the sunset views. At half past three I step into the shower and am in the mood to dress to impress. I embark on a cleansing routine, washing my hair and using all sorts of bath and shower gels I'd been gifted at Christmas over the years. I open a bottle of lotion that says Cocoa Butter. Hmm, smelling edible... Intriguing. I apply it all over my body and feel soft and silky.

I knew it, he's going to get access. Only if he's nice.

I opt for a white maxi dress and a summery look. As I scrub my foot with a pumice stone, exuding glamour from every angle of my being, my phone buzzes. For a second, I wonder if it's Ishaan and imagine what it would be like to say 'yeah, fuck off, thanks'.

Jag: Hey hey! We on for today?
Alia: Yes, see you at—
Jag: I feel quite poorly. Don't think I can make it :(

I stare at the message, then at the time. Half an hour before he would have had to leave his flat, he feels poorly. I am being played again. But I will not be played.

Alia: Take care x

I text him and lock my phone. I set the pumice stone on my nightstand and look at the mess in my room: hairdryer on the dresser, dress on the ironing board, makeup and jewellery strewn across the bed. I am now going to be spending the evening clearing this up.

I am not even disappointed. I am relieved. I envision the rest of the evening. Me in my dressing gown, doner kebab for dinner, bottle of wine, and *Ali G Indahouse* on the telly. This is the new normal. Choosing shit telly over shit men.

Another One Bites the Dust

Being on an online dating app is like being on continuous on-the-job training for a job you aren't sure you even want. Every profile you swipe through, every match you get, every conversation you have teaches you something new about human behaviour, dating protocol, and male-female communication patterns.

I see that nearly everyone I chat to on Clink is broken in some way. There are the fuckboys who are obviously broken in their inherent wiring. Clink almost provides breeding grounds for fuckboys to grow and prosper by having an abundant stock of vulnerable women. I am aware that social media has been calling out fuckboys for the longest time and they're the single biggest target for slander on ladies' nights. One might wonder: If women hate fuckboys so much, why do they keep stepping into fuckboy webs? Well, fuckboys say and do the right things when the opportunity is ripe, and once the woman has been successfully entrapped, they reveal their true colours.

One cannot talk about fuckboys without mentioning the ghosts. The ease of avoiding uncomfortable conversations related to the 'I am just not that into you' variety has made ghosting a phenomenon. The ghosts are, in all manner of speaking, ghosts. They are in your life one minute and gone without a trace the next. Unreachable. Unresponsive. For all intents and purposes, dead to you. Unless they're on your social media. Then they're a slap in your face.

I chat to Meher and Trisha about the ghosts. Trisha finds the entire concept quite unnerving, which isn't surprising. She met her husband during the golden era of organically meeting people, so she never had to try online dating. When she tries to swipe on my app, she ends up swiping in the wrong directions and messes up my matches. I'm almost jealous of how unaware she is of the online dating phenomenon.

'In my time, we met people through friends', Trisha says. 'Does that not work? Can you not meet someone through friends?'

I think about my friends. Apart from Sanjay, there is no one with a known database of male friends that I could potentially get with, and Sanjay has already said no to introducing me to anyone in his circle for fear of me being played by them.

'It's like the Wild West with them, Alia', Sanjay said the one time I asked him. 'Trust me, the second I find someone good enough for you, I will introduce him to you.'

When I ask Meher if she has ever been ghosted, her expression turns into one of agony.

'Ghosting is a bitch, isn't it?' she says.

'So, it's happened to you, then?'

She nods. 'Yeah, once. This guy I went out with before Akash. We went out once, but it was a great date. He was so keen on getting a second date with me and then one day he just stopped replying.'

'Hmm.' I wonder what prompts people to ghost someone. If they didn't find things to be quite what they were expecting, why lie and appear to be keen for another date instead of just being upfront and telling the truth? It doesn't have to be an emotional exchange; the simpler the better. A simple text:

Dear <Name>

Thank you for your time on our date on <day of date>. Although I did enjoy our time together, I'm unsure how I feel about you and so at this stage I will be terminating our communication effective immediately. Should interest arise in the future, I will get back in touch. To unsubscribe, please reply No to this text.

Many thanks, <Your Name>

Or maybe something less formal. Everyone has their own style.

Then there are those who are broken from previous trauma but don't admit it. To be fair, for a Millennial to be on a dating app, some sort of trauma is likely to have occurred. You either met someone in the golden age and it worked out and now you are together, stronger than ever. Or it doesn't work out and leaves you with some level of PTSD.

And then there are people like you and me. Broken from the sheer experience of being on here. But that's not to say it's all gloom and doom. Occasionally a nice guy will come along and you'll get along. Maybe things will work out. Or maybe another one will bite the dust. For me, though, this on-the-job training hasn't been as rewarding as I expected.

Tidings

Everyone gets to the age where it seems that everybody in their real and digital lives is getting engaged, married or pregnant. Meanwhile, I am getting mortified.

But my friends and I have always been quite in keeping with trends, so when the "getting engaged" trend became relevant in our lives, we knew it was going to be no time before one of us announced our entrapment.

One Friday Meher drops a message on the S.A.M text chain asking to meet over the weekend for some news. I immediately text her privately.

Alia: Are you preggo? X
Mehers: LOL no

Not pregnant but wanting to announce something. Could she be moving? Not likely. People move *to* Dubai, not *from* Dubai. Could she have got a new job? Not likely either. She's recently been promoted and been assigned an intern. Someone literally brings her coffee to her desk. She is living the dream. Maybe she wants to meet to celebrate the intern?

But as we sit at the table at the bar Meher has chosen—and brought along a nervous Akash whose hand she is currently holding on to—what she is about to announce becomes increasingly evident.

'Hold up', Sanjay says, looking at them suspiciously. 'Are you two engaged?'

Meher's smile turns into a scowl. 'Fucking hell, Sanj.' She rolls her eyes. 'Yes, we are, but I wanted to say it!'

Akshay chuckles. 'Go on, say it.'

Meher smiles at him, still holding his hand. Then, 'You guys! We're engaged!'

The table erupts into the sounds of 'woo!' and 'wahey!' and 'I'm so happy for you' and 'please don't tell my mum' (that's from me). Meher asks the waiter to take a photo of the group raising glasses of champagne. I can imagine the photo will end up on social media later tonight, possibly with the caption 'A celebration is nothing without friends'.

There are several follow-up questions we need answers to.

When is the wedding and where?

Abu Dhabi in December. We'll have a bachelor/bachelorette trip before the wedding so our close friends will come down a week early and we'll stay on Saadiyat Island.

Is it going to be a super-fancy wedding?

Yes, it's a big, fat Punjabi wedding.

Great. Yes. Fab. A wedding in our group. There is no way I can hide this from my parents, is there? Mum is going to be on my case. 'Alia, even your friends are now getting married. What excuse have you got now?'

'Uh, the lack of decent human beings?' But this answer won't quite cut it.

Fucking hell, Meher, what'd you have to go and get engaged for? Can you just be happy for her please?

We celebrate the happy couple and I realise that with or without Meher's engagement, Mum and Dad are going to worry about my single status, so may as well have some fun and some champagne.

At home, I receive the anticipated phone call. As expected, after the conventional niceties of 'how are you, how's work?' Mum gets straight to the point.

'Have you heard the news?'

'About Meher? Yes, of course I have.'

'So, are you going to the wedding, then?'

'Yes, of course, she's my best friend.'

'Hmm', she says. 'Have you met anyone new recently?'

'No, Mum, there's a distinct lack of decent guys. I think Akash was the last one, in fact', I add jokingly, aware that she is probably not going to take it well but shooting my shot anyway.

'Hmm', she says again. 'What about Sanjay?'

'What about Sanjay?' I ask her cautiously.

'You've known Sanjay for a long time', she says. 'And we like him too. Have you ever thought about marrying him?'

I pause. And then I laugh. 'No, Mother', I say. 'I have not thought about marrying Sanj.'

'Why, what's wrong with him?'

'There's nothing wrong with him, I just don't feel that way about him. And he doesn't feel that way about me.'

'Such a lovely boy.' I imagine her shaking her head. 'You know love dies down, right? It's the companionship and the compatibility that remains. If you and Sanjay are compatible, think about it.'

'I think you might be the most romantic person I have ever known.'

I wonder if Meher's mother has ever said this to her about Akash, that their love will die down at some point and what will remain will be compatibility and companionship. Indian parents don't usually do toasts at their kids' weddings, but if they did, I'd like to watch what sort of reaction that particular statement would garner.

Mum and Dad could choose not to be stressed about my life just because Meher is getting married. If stress could work that way, it would be lovely. If the human mind wasn't programmed to find the grass on the other side greener, life would certainly be more blissful. Mum and Dad wouldn't think me being married would be better than me being single. How can they compare me to Meher? Meher has been clear about what she wants and with whom for a long time now. Me, on the other hand? I have never been clear about either of these things. My mind hasn't even started going there. I go on Clink dates for the sake of going on dates so that if someone tolerable comes along, I won't miss it. But that's not what Meher has with Akash. Meher is marrying Akash. She doesn't find him tolerable. She finds him... adorable. They love each other.

For fuck's sake, what am I even doing on Clink? Waiting for someone tolerable? Waiting for the Ishaans of the world to tempt me with their scent and humour and good looks and then ghost me after they've invaded my garden? Waiting for the Jags of the world to chicken out? Waiting for the Davids to make me feel like I might be important to them but learn that the opposite is true within a few weeks? Perhaps I should have better standards. Perhaps I shouldn't be going out with Tom, Dick, *and* Harry.

What do I even want? I haven't the faintest. Is that bad? It isn't bad, is it? Well, by Mum and Dad's standards, yes, it's bad, but I don't think it's bad. Is it truly terrible if I don't know what my purpose is? I suppose I have an inkling of what my purpose is, of what I want from my life. I want peace. I want everybody in my life to chill the fuck out and let me chill out. That's it, that's what I want: to chill. I want Mum and Dad to not find the news of Meher's engagement stressful, but rather be happy that she has found what she was looking for, and to help me find what I'm looking for: chill.

Does everybody spiral like that when their best friend gets engaged?

The Wedding Party

I have always maintained that Abu Dhabi is a gorgeous location. So when we arrive at Saadiyat Island for the pre-wedding bachelorette trip, I am glad that everyone seems in awe of it.

The bridal party has come downstairs to the lobby of our gloriously beautiful hotel to greet Akash's friends from Nottingham, who all went to med school together and I imagine would all be on every Indian Aunty's radar as a match for their unwed daughter, including my own mother's scanning eye for her unwed daughter, i.e., me.

Whether it's by virtue of them being doctors or the fact that they're the groom's friends is uncertain to me, but they have been receiving VIP treatment since they arrived about twenty minutes ago. Indian weddings are primarily about keeping the groom and his troops happy, I know this, but watching Akash's and Meher's parents coming downstairs to greet them is proving this point to a great degree.

When the bride's friends arrived, Meher hurriedly said hello before rushing off to take a phone call. In stark contrast, the groom's friends are being offered welcome beverages in the form of jasmine-flavoured iced tea, and a porter is carrying their IDs to the check-in desk for them so they can relax in the lobby.

This gives me and Sanjay and the rest of Meher's friends enough time to stand in the background and comment on 'the boys'.

There are always five types of groom's friends at any wedding: a) the friend using the opportunity to pull. Most of them fall into this category; b) the friend who sticks around for the open bar and uses it to its maximum capacity to the best of his ability; c) the one good-looking guy who's going to be the target of every Aunty in the wedding party; d) the guy who will most likely vanish before the actual wedding ceremony, which is quite a solemn and religious affair, and reappear for the wedding reception, and e) the token non-Indian guy. This guy gets the most special treatment because he's going to spread the word about how incredible and colourful Indian weddings are.

Akash's friends show signs of all these categories. There's Jack, the token white guy, who is currently sipping tea and occasionally expressing how delicious it is and how it's his first Indian wedding and how he can't wait to see what a traditional wedding looks like. He wants to wear traditional Indian apparel and eat Indian food and dance to Indian tunes. I'm sure he'll be part of the groom's dance recital at the *Sangeet*[15] ceremony later and I can't wait to see him dancing off-beat to Punjabi songs.

Next to Jack is Pav, whose name is as common among the Punjabi fuckboys of the world as Punjabis are in Southall.

15   One of the many parties at an Indian wedding. Traditionally it was where the women of the house would sing traditional folk songs for the bride. Today, it's everyone singing everything to everyone and dancing like there's no tomorrow.

Pav looks like he's going to be on the pull at every party and will not rest until he has found someone worthy of his attention. He has already eyed me in a rather creepy way, and by way of my resting bitch face I have made clear that I am not interested.

There's Krish, who is attractive not only through his medical degree but also through his geek chic persona, so you just know that in addition to making all the Aunties cream their knickers, he is going to raise eyebrows amongst Meher's female friends. I myself eye Krish a few times, at which Sanjay rolls his eyes. The idea that Sanjay is not the only good-looking guy at the wedding is not going down well with him.

There's TJ, who has checked into the hotel in a drunken stupor thanks to duty-free alcohol, and who has been yelling out Meher's name since arriving at the hotel. 'Meher! You're making Akash so happy, which means you're making me so happy', he says. I don't expect to see TJ at the actual wedding ceremony. I expect him to be lying face down on the floor next to his bed in his hotel room, still in his clothes from the previous night and then doing the walk of shame into the banquet hall soon after the wedding.

The first of many pre-parties is tonight. I am curious to see how many of my guesses and categories are accurate.

When the chaos from multiple people checking in at the same time dies down, Meher walks up to me and Sanjay with a heavy sigh. Poor thing. I can't imagine having to bear wedding stress as a bride is easy.

'Is that all of them?' Sanjay says.

'No, there's one more. He's checking in but he's quiet', Meher says as she rubs her eyes.

I nod. 'How are you feeling?'

A pause from her. 'Stressed', she admits. 'But, no, we'll have fun tonight. This lot, though', she adds with a small roll of her eyes, 'they're fucking mental.'

'Yeah, I mean', I say, 'were you expecting one of *your* friends to be the crazy one?'

'Yeah, we met at the Bright Students' Club', Sanjay adds matter-of-factly. I chuckle at this little piece of our history that continues to amuse us. 'We were never going to be the crazy ones.'

Meher smiles. 'Alright, I'm going to head up', she says. 'See you in two hours. Don't forget to look your sexiest', she adds with a wink.

As Meher walks away, I rustle through my purse for cigarettes.

'Okay, if you're going to do that', Sanjay says, 'I'm going to head up too.'

'Wow, way to leave a friend alone!' I protest jokingly.

I walk outside and light up my cigarette, the cool breeze brushing against my face. It's a quiet evening, barring the sound of incoming cars at the hotel entrance. I think about the week coming up, which is literally lined up with parties. The party tonight is a welcome party by the pool. Tomorrow is a yacht party with just Meher and her friends. We have decided to grace the range at the local golf course with our presence and our shitty golf skills on one day as well, heading to the clubhouse after that for a classy drink. More parties. And then comes the wedding, which is a collection of parties as well.

The wedding usually starts with the engagement ceremony where the bride and groom exchange rings after the families have said a prayer. This is followed by a party. The next day starts with the *Mehndi*[16] ceremony, followed by lunch and then a full-fledged party in the evening in the form of the Sangeet. This tends to get quite messy with the drinking and dancing, which is why not a lot of people are expected to appear at the wedding the following morning, which, in Meher's case, is scheduled for nine o'clock.

I watch my cigarette burning out. It reminds me of Raj and how his little statement 'someone as beautiful as you shouldn't smoke' had prompted me to toss it into the water. My romantic feelings for Raj have mostly died down, but I do occasionally wonder what life would have been like if Raj had kissed me because of feelings instead of my dress.

I head back into the hotel, aware that I now smell like an ashtray. There is smoke in my hair and in my hands; I blame the poor quality of cigarettes in the hotel mini mart. I walk up to the elevators where a man stands waiting. He looks at me and looks back at the lift and then again at me. He subtly takes a whiff of the air around him.

I smile, embarrassed. And then I can't stop myself.

'I'm sorry', I say, 'can you kind of tell I've just had a smoke?'

He turns to look at me again, looking calm and almost dazed. 'I can.'

'Right. Sorry about that.'

'It's alright, I kind of wish I had one now.'

16   Ceremony to apply henna on the bride's hands. The bride and groom's female friends and family usually also apply henna designs on their hands here.

I shrug and retrieve the pack I have in my purse and offer it to him.

'No, no, I shouldn't!' he says with a chuckle. 'I'm a doctor. Technically it's against my religion.'

Fucking hell, this place is filled with doctors.

'Are you a friend of Akash's?' I ask with a small frown.

'Yes! Are you from the wedding as well?' He has an Indian accent but sounds strangely polished, like he possibly belongs to royalty in India.

'Yes, I'm a friend of Meher's.'

'Ah, nice to meet you!' he says, extending his hand for me to shake. 'I'm Kabir.'

'Alia.'

'Right', he says, when the elevator opens up on his floor. 'I'll see you at the party then.'

The Pull Party

When Meher said that the first party in the 'Akash weds Meher' soiree was a pool party, I assumed it would be quite a chilled-out affair with mellow RnB in the background. I envisioned that after a few drinks the RnB would transform into Punjabi music and at least one person—my bet was TJ—would fall into the pool, causing a massive splash, potentially alerting management and the parents of the bride and the groom.

The actual party is far beyond my imagination. The female serving staff double as Brazilian dancers, so any time an upbeat song comes on, the servers stand on the stools lining the internal circumference of the pool and break into a very cheerleader style of dance. The boys are having a wonderful time objectifying these women.

The male performers have been employed to undertake a fire show. I can't help but wonder why the men get to leer at female dancers twerking away while the women get to watch a fire show.

I can see why Meher asked us to dress in our sexiest. Literally everyone at the party is decked up in shimmery clothes and those in the pool have even found shimmery bikinis. I am in a red shimmery playsuit that ties around my neck, highlighting my collarbone and shoulders. My hair is up in a bun so it doesn't interfere with my engagement with the endless flow of cocktails.

The music is blaring, the dancing is as far from elegant as humanly possible, and the banter is abounding. The celebration has started in true big, fat Punjabi wedding style.

As the night progresses, I see that TJ has created quite the ruckus already, trying to prompt the DJ to play the music of Badshah[17] and the DJ refusing (thank the Lord for that). My guess that he will be quite the destructive mess might be accurate. I look at the rest of the group and wonder if Jack is disappointed that nothing about this Brazilian pool bash is traditionally Indian and if he was expecting an elephant to show up. Akash and the rest of the boys are engaging in lad behaviour, and everyone seems to be having a good time.

The bridal party take over the dance floor unanimously as tunes like "Jump Around" blare across the massive pool. We are exactly the image we had expected we would be. Sanjay's foot has been nearly trampled by a high-heeled shoe, and my playsuit has been soaked with someone else's drink.

I take a moment to regain my composure and head to the bar at the back that is serving the restaurant. It is reasonably far from the pool party so the music is quieter and I can have a moment of peace. I grab some tissues and another drink, and as I pat myself dry, I very nearly crash into Kabir.

'Oh!' I jump. 'Dr. Kabir.'

Kabir smiles. 'I'm not on call right now, you can call me Kabir.'

I look at him for a second. 'No.' I shake my head. 'It's Dr. Kabir.'

17   Indian rap artist

Are you starting to subscribe to the Indian ideology of 'doctor is better'?

'What are you drinking?' he says, leaning with his back against the bar.

'Gin and tonic.'

He grins. 'That's a basic ass drink.'

He turns to face the bartender and while he places his order, I take a look at him, at his person. He looks comfortably dressed in white shorts and a light blue shirt that hugs his body flatteringly. His arms are bulging under his sleeves and his back and shoulders are quite broad. If ever there was a 'manly' man, this was it. His hair is neatly gelled back and a light stubble adorns his face.

'Right', I say when he's done chatting to the bartender. 'I'm gonna head back.' I am suddenly overcome with a shy awkwardness.

'Oh, no, don't go', he says with a smile. 'I was only joking.'

I pause. A smile. Then, 'No, you weren't.'

'No, I wasn't.' He grins again. 'It *is* a basic ass drink.'

'And you, an Indian man with your whiskey, that's not basic at all', I say sarcastically.

Kabir laughs.

'Would you care to sit for a minute?' he says. 'I need a break from that crowd.'

He follows me to a set of sofas around a table, with a view of the madness within the party. One of the Brazilian dancers is now performing a champagne shower. The last time I'd been at a champagne shower, I got champagne in my eyes and my contact lenses burnt like hell. Hip-happening just doesn't agree with me sometimes.

'What do you think of this venue?'

'Oh, are we going to do small talk?' I say. Tipsy Alia is currently in charge of my speech.

Kabir grins. 'You're quite cheeky, aren't you?'

'No, just a little tipsy.'

There is something in his smile, in the carefree aura he exudes, that makes me a bit self-conscious. I feel like his eyes are scanning me thoroughly and I don't know what he sees.

'How long have you known Meher?' he asks casually.

'We went to school together. I've known her practically all my life. How long have you known Akash?'

'We went to uni together, so about... Gah, has it been seven years already?!'

'Yes, time flies. My Facebook memories showed me that three years ago today I was at my postgrad graduation ceremony.'

'So, you're a postgrad then?'

'Yes.'

'What did you study?'

'Financial law.'

'Boring.'

'Thanks.' I chuckle. 'You're a doctor?'

'Yes, ma'am. Dermatologist. Any rashes you'd like me to check out?' he adds with a grin.

'Not for now, thanks', I say slowly, also starting to grin.

'Maybe we need to get you another drink then.'

What is happening? Who is this man? Dr. Kabir. *Are we flirting?* It would appear so.

'So, Dr. Kabir', I say. 'Why are you here? Why aren't you with the boys?'

'Half of them are in the process of passing out, and the other half are with their girlfriends.'

'And... you don't have a girlfriend?' I say with a small smile, subtly—or so I thought—taking a chance.

'My girlfriend is back home in Mumbai.'

My smile vanishes. 'Ah.'

'I'm joking.' Kabir grins, taking a sip of his drink, leaning toward me. 'But nice to know you were slightly disappointed.'

'You're a cheeky man.'

'I can be.'

Seriously, what the fuck is happening? Sometimes I want to chill, not constantly be on my toes for when you fuck up with yet another man.

'No, seriously', I continue. 'Why are you here? Why aren't you with the boys?'

'The boys are boring. You're not boring', he says softly. 'Thought I might chat to you. Get to know you.'

Alia, why are we being dumb? He's trying to pull. Don't get pulled in, please, I really just want to chill.

As time goes on I can sense him sliding closer, but I don't mind. Sassy does, for a change, but I don't. I am three double gins down now anyway, so the concept of inhibitions is foreign to me. We chat about his hometown, Mumbai. I tell him I generally find Mumbai and people from Mumbai to be quite snooty and full of themselves, and he pretends to be upset.

'You just haven't met the right people', he says. 'Mumbai is a great place. You should visit some time.'

'Yeah, that's not happening', I say.

He tells me about the haunts in Mumbai that offer the best street food, about the Gateway of India that has been the backdrop for photos for everyone visiting since time immemorial, and about how the city has a rich culture and history, something I would be able to see if I give it a chance. I seriously think about planning a trip but change my mind quite quickly when I remember my last trip to India.

'Firstly, I just want to say, no offense is meant to India through this story', I start.

Kabir laughs. 'Go on, then, what made your last trip so traumatic?'

'It was my sister's wedding shopping trip. It was literally the worst.'

'Where did you go?'

I recount the tale of navigating the tiny corners of the oldest parts of New Delhi and how I got nearly crashed into by a rickshaw from behind because the women in front of me refused to move and clear the way for it.

Kabir laughs again.

We continue to chat about our work. He tells me stories about the strangest things he has encountered in his practice and I tell him about how I want to be the cleverest academic known to mankind through my research.

About forty-five minutes later my phone rings loudly, disturbing our peace.

'Yes, Sanj?' I answer.

'Where are you? Did we lose you?' he screams into the phone.

'No, I'm just at the bar in the restaurant, at the far end.'

'What are you doing there?!'

'Getting a drink.'

'Come back! We miss you!'

'Yeah, coming.'

I hang up. 'That's my call to leave', I say, turning to face Kabir.

He nods. 'Will I see you again?'

'We're in the same hotel for the next ten days. I don't see why you won't see me again.'

'Well, you could always avoid me', he says, lightly brushing my hair away from my face.

'I don't want to', I say with a small smile.

He leans forward, one hand tucking my hair behind an ear and pulling my face slightly toward him, and kisses me softly.

Fucking hell, Alia, I told you not to get pulled in. Um... sorry, not sorry?

Holiday Romance

Sexual chemistry, banter, and ground rules. These are the key ingredients for a successful holiday romance. The previous night went to show that sexual chemistry and banter are not lacking with Kabir, but if I want to try my hand at a holiday romance, I need to establish ground rules with myself. Not him. He and I both know that we probably won't see each other again. It's my naive mind that needs the ground rules. Well, singular rule, really. Don't fall for the man.

I wake up moderately hungover but glad that I had the presence of mind to place a bottle of water on my nightstand. After downing a litre of water I feel awake enough to do what we all do every morning: scroll through social media. And the first notification to brighten up my morning is *'bajwa.kabir has started following you - 53m ago.'* The next is *'bajwa.kabir liked your photo - 53m ago'*.

I grin and open his profile. His last post is from three years ago of a sunset in Morocco, with his back facing the camera. There are pictures of him with his family, some from a desert safari in the Hatta desert. Clearly this isn't his first trip to the UAE. I debate whether or not I should scroll further. I feel like scrolling down uncovers past truths that I don't really need to know. Once, I stalked a man to such depths of the internet that I uncovered pictures of him with a soul patch and I could never go out with him again.

I resolve not to explore his profile. I don't know what this is. Are we going to see each other again? Probably. Do we pretend last night didn't happen? Don't know. Are we going to have one-on-one conversations like last night again? Don't know. Am I attracted to him? Don't know. Some things I do know, though. Like, is he a sex bomb? Little bit. Quite a bit, actually.

My thoughts are interrupted by the sound of another notification.

Kabir: Thinking about you x

I can't help but smile, but almost instantly, Sassy interrupts. *This has Ishaan written all over it.* What do you mean? *Ishaan told us he was thinking about us but all he wanted to do was shag us and never call us again.* Would that be so bad with Kabir? He lives in India, I live in Dubai. This doesn't exactly have 'long-term' written across it. *Fine, your funeral.*

I grin at the message again and hit the cursor.

Alia: Liar

Oh, we're allowed to be sassy? Yes, I told you. We can screw up here. Literally, no consequence. He could be an Ishaan, but it doesn't matter. He's going back to India; he can't ghost us.

Kabir: You don't believe me?
Alia: How can I? I don't know you, do I?

Kabir: Well, we must remedy that.
Alia: How do you suggest we do that?
Kabir: Dinner?
Alia: Why not
Kabir: 7:30? The restaurant by the beach?
Alia: Sounds good x

As I head to the bathroom, it occurs to me that I have just done what I couldn't do for the past two years. I bagged a date who asked me out organically. No dating apps, no matrimonial apps. And it took a man from another country to do that. Fucking hell. I am jubilant and pissed off in equal measure. Is there really such a shortage of decent men in Dubai that an actual tourist has to take me out and text me things like *Thinking of you x*? And I can't even be excited, because if he turns out to be incredible and everything I could ever want, I can't hope for a future with him. Universe, you bitch, you've done it again. My mood has transformed from slightly flirtatious to fucking pissed within moments.

I calm down quickly though. I don't know if Kabir is going to be a good guy. He could be a dick. He could fall in the dick percentile of the dating world. Statistically, that is the most likely scenario. So perhaps I have nothing to worry about. Perhaps the Universe is being kind to me. Perhaps the Universe just wants to give Nether Alia some relief. I didn't realise the Universe could care this much.

I head down to the pool where Meher and Akash are continuing the pool party into the day in an unofficial capacity. The shiny, shimmery bikinis are still out in the sun and the men with their abs are strutting around. I set my towel on a sunbed and as I apply sunblock, realise this is what I had hoped to do at Meher's wedding—chill out. Chilling by the pool in a fancy-ass hotel is more relaxing than stressing out about an accidental date with a friend of the groom.

But I can't help myself. As I've said before, being in the dating market has broken me to the extent that something like a casual date cannot be experienced without overthinking things and going slightly mad.

I could just go into this date without any expectations. Wouldn't that be nice? It really would. Imagine that. Imagine a date where you could literally be your worst self and nothing bad could happen because you know there is no future. If I get a positive outcome from the date, well, fab. If not, it's not like I was expecting a date at the wedding in the first place, so it's like nothing happened.

I am wrong to stress out. I should be excited. This is my chance to experience a no-pressure date.

My mood transforms from 'fucking pissed' to slightly flirtatious again and I join Meher and the rest of the group as they groove to the sound of "Lady Hear Me Tonight".

Let's Get It On

I am quite calm as I get dressed for my big date with Kabir. I call it a big date, but it could come crashing down as the biggest downer of a date. That is the beauty of the situation. Anything can happen.

But that isn't to say that I'm not nervous about seeing him again. He had quite the presence last night. He was relaxed and calm, but his eyes peered through mine, as if he was looking into a window and peering into my very soul. Dramatic, right? Hence, the nerves.

I'm nervous about another kiss. The kiss last night was short, but it was... powerful. You know how sometimes less is more? It was true with his kiss. It was like being drugged for a few seconds and then coming back to reality. So, yes, I am nervous about seeing him again.

I settle for a black-and-white maxi dress for this dinner date at the restaurant by the beach. It's a pleasant change from glamming up for a date at a fancy new Business Bay venue. This is nice.

I walk up to the restaurant at half past seven and find him at the table. I smile. Of course he's already here. Of course Kabir is the one who doesn't make me wait. Universe, you feisty bitch.

'I'm so sorry, were you waiting long?' I say as I approach him.

'No, you're fine', he says, stroking my arm lightly, broad smile on his face and kissing my cheek.

He smiles as I sit and I smile back, inwardly admiring how he looks. I like how comfortable he looks, this time in a blue Aztec-print shirt and beige shorts. The entire setting is of comfort, with the sound of the waves, the hint of sun on our faces from tanning at the pool this afternoon, and the acoustic guitar playing Mediterranean sounds in the background. If I could leave Kabir a review somewhere, I would give him a 10/10 on choice of venue and timekeeping.

We order drinks and settle into conversation. Kabir finds it fascinating that life in this surreal land is my life every day.

'So, the things we did this afternoon at the pool. You do that every weekend?'

'Well, not every weekend.' I shrug. 'But we do have the ability to do it.'

'That's mad!'

He tells me about his holiday in Dubai many years ago and how the city has probably changed since then. I pretend that I haven't stalked his social media account a little bit and that his Dubai trip is news to me.

As our food and drinks arrive, banter and laughter seem to be abounding again.

'So, what's dating like in Dubai?' he says. 'If you're single, I have to imagine it isn't great at the moment?'

I chuckle. 'It's… horrific. But I imagine it's horrific everywhere.'

'What are you looking for?'

'Well, nothing too complicated. I literally just want a man who can make me laugh with his wit and humour', I say. 'So far I have only met men who make me laugh at them, not with them.'

Kabir chuckles. 'Yeah, I know what you mean. It's hard to find.'

'And you? What are you looking for?'

'Just someone I get along with. Someone I can banter with. There's no one in Mumbai and my search seems to have brought me to the deserts of the Middle East, where... I seem to be getting along with you.'

I chuckle.

Maybe we do need ground rules.

'Why don't you tell me about your life in Mumbai?' I say.

'Nice dodge,' he says with a grin.

When we get the bill Kabir proposes a walk along the beach and then on to the hotel. As we walk, chatting away, our hands brushing against each other, I imagine what it would be like if he was to hold my hand. I have never experienced the hand-holding phenomenon that couples the world over seem to be so deeply involved in. I have always found it to be far more intimate than anything else, even sex. Sex can be brought on by passion, but handholding comes from a level of affection I have never experienced.

The last time I imagined holding someone's hand was with Ishaan. The ghost. So the memory of that vision makes me cringe. Thinking about holding Kabir's hand doesn't make me cringe.

It is a pleasant sound, laughter mixed with waves. It sounds like happiness. Like joy in its purest form, where nothing outside Meher's wedding bubble can touch us. I actively restrain myself from thinking about how depressing going back to Dubai will be.

As we enter the hotel, Kabir looks at me. 'So, would you like to get a drink in my room?' He smiles with an endearing earnestness.

'It's the oldest trick in the book, Kabir', I say, jokingly rolling my eyes. 'But yes, I'd like that.'

When he opens the door to his room, I see that he has been given an upgrade to a suite.

'Whoa', I say, walking to the window and placing my hands on the windowsill. 'This is a beautiful view. You can see the sea!'

'Yeah, it looks much better in the morning, actually', he says walking up behind me. 'So, you'll need to stay until tomorrow morning to be able to see that.'

I grin and then suddenly realise what's about to happen when I feel his hands wrapping around my waist. He plants soft kisses on my shoulder and neck and I turn to face him with a smile. He kisses me, engulfing me in his tight embrace. I wish we had a vinyl record of Marvin Gaye's "Let's Get it On" in the room. The mood doesn't require any more setting, but it would be hilarious.

A Whole New World

In the show *Miranda* on BBC Two, Miranda's friend and shop manager, Stevie Sutton, often holds up a placard with Heather Small's picture on it and does an immaculate impression of her singing "Proud". She asks 'What have you done today to make you feel proud?' and then lists the achievements of the day that she is particularly proud of.

Waking up in Kabir's bed next to him, I can hear Heather Small's voice in my head asking, 'What have you done today to make you feel proud?' *Today, Heather, I woke up next to a stranger and I'm strangely proud of it, even though he did most of the work.*

I turn to look at Kabir's face. He's sleeping peacefully and breathing heavily. I'm glad he isn't a snorer. I can't imagine being this attracted to him if he was a snorer. Is that why the chemistry dies in a relationship as you spend more time with the partner? Is that what Mum and Dad are always on about?

It's still only six o'clock in the morning. For someone on holiday, this is not the time I should be waking up at. But sleep eludes me in a strange bed, no matter how comfortable I feel. It's dark outside but I can just see the waves hitting up against the shore through the window. The magic window that Kabir thought he could use to lure me into his bedroom. In the end, as we know, he really needn't have tried that hard. Just asking, 'you wanna?' would have been enough.

I think back to the many, many dates I have been on. Many, many first dates, fewer second dates, and barely any third dates. I think back to the IndianRishtaa guys. There was no chemistry there. There was barely any conversation. I think back to Harjit Dhaliwal who could barely stay in the same cafe as me for a solid fifteen minutes before scuttling away like a rat. There was literally nothing there, not even a coffee.

I think back to the Ishaans and the Jags and the many, many others from Clink. There was some chemistry there. But there was something missing. The desire to make an effort, maybe? When was the last time I went on a date where a man made a reservation at a restaurant, showed up five minutes early, and had proper banter and laughter with me? That shouldn't be such a high bar, but unfortunately it is.

I reach for my phone and find several unread messages. Messages on the S.A.M group to say that Sanjay is going out with Akash's boys, on the bridal party group to say that breakfast will be served from seven until eleven, from my family, from work, and one from Kabir that I had only read the preview of, that said *Sat at the back x.*

Since receiving that, every other message has been unimportant, irrelevant even. Why do I care that Sanjay is going out with the boys? I don't. Maybe it's holiday goggles. Maybe it's knowing that there is no consequence to anything that makes everything seem delightful.

I revisit the night in my mind. His touch was so passionate, so urgent. How? Why? How does it happen that after knowing someone for only an evening, you get this urge to be with them

210

in the most intimate way? I think back to the middle of the night when I woke up because he wrapped his arm around my waist, resting his head on my chest. I held on to him like a mother cradling a baby. It felt strange. And lovely.

Kabir is still deeply asleep, so I get out of bed and into the bathroom. My reflection in the mirror is dishevelled. Hair a mess, cakey makeup on my face. Aside from that, I look exactly as I did last night. But I feel different. I feel confused. Happy as well, of course, because coitus leads to happy hormones, but also confused.

What happens now? Do we pretend like nothing happened and get on with our holiday? Do we keep this a secret from our friends? Covering up the date had been hard work last night. I'd insisted I had a bad back from sleeping weird and desperately needed a massage and rest and hence would not be able to join everyone as they painted the town red. God only knows what Kabir said. I have a feeling Sanjay is already suspicious. He is annoyed anyway that I seem to have dumped him on our little trip; any more absences will prompt him to ask questions, and I might break.

I wash my face and grab an unused dental kit. I consider making a quiet escape to my room, but I also don't want this to look like I feel I made a mistake. It was definitely not a mistake.

I don't want to walk back into the bedroom. When Kabir wakes up, we'll have an awkward morning-after conversation, which I'm not particularly keen on. It is not actually possible, but I do also have a feeling he might find a way to ghost me. Maybe it's Ishaan/David PTSD and I'm being crazy, but it is a real fear.

When I do walk out of the bathroom, Kabir is awake, sitting up in bed, hands behind his head, looking relaxed. Always so relaxed. Where can I find his level of zen?

He looks at me and smiles. It's a beautiful smile.

'Morning, gorgeous', he says, and I have the strongest urge to jump on the bed and kiss him, only deterred by the prospect of morning breath.

'Coffee?' he says, slipping out of the covers.

'Yes, please', I say and he puts the kettle on. He slips his hands around my waist and kisses my cheek from behind. Maybe he's conscious of morning breath too.

'You still smell incredible', he says with a hoarse morning voice.

I chuckle. 'It's cocoa butter', I say. 'I wanted to smell edible.'

'Naughty.'

He walks into the bathroom and the water boils. I prepare two cups of coffee and walk out onto the balcony to see what the weather is like. It is a perfect morning to lounge in the sun. Well, every morning is perfect for that. But if I'm going to be overthinking for the rest of the day, I would rather have the sun for company. When I walk back inside, Kabir is putting on his shirt.

'What are your plans for today?'

'Probably just go to the pool with Meher', I say.

'And will you be posting bikini pictures online?'

I smile. 'Don't be creepy.'

'Well, I need something to keep me going until I see you later.'

'Later?'

'Unless you don't want to?'

'I want to', I say slowly.

He smiles. 'Good', he says. 'I think we get along, don't you?'

'I do.'

'I'm a bit annoyed at the logistics', he continues. 'Why don't you live in Mumbai?'

'Because it's a shithole.'

He laughs. 'I think I need a few more dates with you.'

'Well, I'm sure that can be arranged', I say slowly.

'You seem confused.'

'I am, a little.'

Kabir sighs and sits down on the bed. 'I know we're going to go back to our separate lives', he says, 'but I'd hate to miss the opportunity to get to know you and spend time with you just because we live in different countries.'

I pause. Then, 'You make it sound like it isn't as big a logistical issue as it sounds.'

Kabir chuckles. 'It is, but I'm a fucking idiot and I like you. Fuck me.' He sighs and chuckles again.

We did fuck you last night. Pretty solid. Always keeping it classy, Sassy.

I don't know what to make of this unexpected declaration of feelings. He could be lying. He could very possibly be lying. Maybe he thinks that's what I want to hear to continue his supply of holiday shenanigans, but he really needn't bother. He could just say 'I'd like to keep hooking up without consequence' and I'd be okay with that. Kabir can sense my lack of trust, I can see that. But this is a world we're both unfamiliar with. A world where you can potentially speak the truth without having to worry about consequence. We might have just died and come back to life in Utopia instead of Abu Dhabi.

The Beautiful Bubble

In a very basic bitch style, I have ended up making Meher's wedding all about my serious-casual relationship. It is casual because we know there's an end date to our shenanigans and so developing serious feelings is not an option, but it is also serious in that we do actually like each other, if we are to believe each other's words. How or why this has happened is anybody's guess—maybe the Universe is itching to act up again—but it has happened and there's not much we can do about it.

What I should be doing though, is focusing on my trust issues. I am a Millennial so acknowledging and accepting my trauma is now more socially acceptable than it ever was, but I am also an Indian Millennial, which means I can hear my ancestors in my head: *Anxiety and trauma are fancy words. Mental health is a farce. Be grateful for what you have.* I can't imagine telling my parents that I don't wish to date yet because I am riddled with trust issues. I can picture them staring at me and then pointing at my face and laughing, saying, 'No, seriously, why don't you want to date?'

The past few days have been excellent, though. There's really no other way to describe it. Maybe shagadelic? Shagadellically excellent.

My mornings start with Kabir and cuddles. I never knew cuddling was so great. Not finding someone tolerable enough on Clink to cuddle with has robbed me of so many cuddles. I've made up for it this week though.

The bride and groom and all the friends go for a swim and then get breakfast together, adding a splash of Baileys to our coffees to kickstart the day. We bathe in the glory of the sun and head out for touristy activities; nothing too intense, something simple like visiting the Grand Mosque. We come back to the hotel and head to one of the parties that Meher and Akash have planned for us. Really, planning so many parties for their friends to get drunk and pull—truly, the most generous friends anyone could ask for and the biggest, fattest Punjabi wedding I have ever witnessed.

After the parties, Kabir and I sneak into one of our rooms for a shagadellically excellent experience of our own. We chat, we laugh, we kiss, we recount childhood tales with nostalgia... and then I kill my own buzz by asking myself why we are doing this.

Maybe not everything has a purpose. Maybe some experiences are just experiences. I have no connection to Mumbai and Kabir has no connection with Dubai. That things have to end as soon as the wedding is over could not be more obvious.

Is Kabir the perfect companion? I don't know. What I do know is that when I am with him, my entire being feels... different. I've known him for only a few days but I wonder if the length of time two people have known each other is a good estimate of the connection they might have.

Chemistry fails me. I don't understand it one bit. What defines chemistry between two people? I have tried to know several people at the level I have come to know Kabir at, but spending a few days with them only made me feel frustrated enough to hit my head against a wall. Why is Kabir not that kind of person? What sets him apart?

Is this the best thing in the world? Or is it the worst thing in the world? That we can be free with each other for a week, completely free, no limits to what we can do or say, without any consequence. Would we always choose this over a long-term relationship where we have to think and think about the consequences of our actions and words? Should we get into all relationships with a contract mindset?

And why is it that physical boundaries exist between me and Kabir? Why is the Universe *this* catty? I find someone decent, and he likes me and I like him too, but I can't have him beyond our brief fairy tale.

I am swirling into a whirlpool of emotions. There's happiness in his company, comfort in his embrace, warmth in his touch, and ecstasy in his arms. Losing myself in feelings for him makes me feel drunk. And I'm not sure how much I like losing control. And there's anticipated sadness, knowing he is not to be mine, and frustration that whoever comes next will be second best. Comparison is the thief of joy, and I'm about to turn into the biggest burglar of my own brain.

So maybe this is it. I should tell Mum and Dad that the search is over. I found the one. He lives in India though, so that's not going to happen.

Despite the fretting, I'm happy in this bubble. The bubble gets closer to bursting each day, but the bubble is so beautiful I could serenade it with a poem. So beautiful that its beauty distracts me from its inevitable end.

The End of Akash's Freedom—and other sexist jokes

Here we are. The end of the road. Well, technically it's the beginning of Meher and Akash's lives as 'Meher and Akash' as opposed to 'Meher' and 'Akash', but for the guests it's literally the end of the road. The official bursting of the bubble ceremony, or as they call it on their wedding invite, the wedding ceremony or *Anand Karaj*.

As expected, the Gurdwara is not busy at nine o'clock in the morning. Meher's close friends have been instructed to arrive on time to ensure that Meher has company while she waits for Akash. You would think that the bride and groom and the entire wedding party would be at the wedding venue at the time set for the wedding, but an Indian wedding transcends all sense of time.

Nine o'clock is just what the invitation says. That's when the bride gets to the venue, but the groom and his friends and family won't be at the venue then. No, they'll take their sweet time. Guests will start arriving about an hour after the bride is already there. The priests will question where the groom is. Then, maybe, the groom will arrive by eleven, or even half past eleven. The nine o'clock time could be considered simply as filler for the empty space on the card.

At half past eleven on Thursday morning, we watch Meher and Akash walking in circles around the Sikh holy book, the *Guru Granth Sahib*. Meher's mother has been handed official paperwork by the Gurdwara committee, which she has now handed to me to complete. I am frantically filling it out, head bent earnestly over the papers, occasionally looking up to watch the beautiful couple. Meher is dressed in a red *lehenga*[18] with gold designs all over it, and Akash is walking ahead of her in a beige *sherwani*[19], head adorned with a red turban. They do make a lovely couple.

I hand the paperwork in and catch sight of my mother in the distance watching the couple, tearing up a little. I look at the women around her. They are all silently weeping. I remember my mother describing this particular moment when she got married. Four circles around the book later, she had transformed into Mrs. Arora. Her life had changed. She had said goodbye to her parents and her siblings. They were no longer hers. 'But surely, they're still your family', I countered. 'Yes', she said, 'but marriage changes you.'

She told me how everything becomes formal in the relationship between her and her parents, that they would now treat her differently, as if she was no longer a part of their family but a guest every time she visited. She told me that life was no

18   Traditional Indian women's outfit
19   Traditional Indian men's outfit

longer about her previous family but her new family. Watching any wedding ceremony going forward made her cry just as she did at her own wedding because she was watching someone else's life change.

'And you want this for me, why?'

'Meher is getting married', she said. 'Soon, Sanjay will too. All your other friends will find their partners at some point. How long do you think you can stay on your own?'

I didn't have an answer then and I don't have an answer now, but it still confounds me that there is a room full of crying women, almost lamenting how their lives changed after getting married but still insisting their children go after that life. Of course, that was a twentieth-century phenomenon and parents today will insist that relationships have changed in the Millennial age, but it still surprises me.

I turn to take a look at the men, none of whom is showing any sign any remorse. Of course they aren't. How did their life change after getting married? Sure, they got a wife, an actual real-life person in their lives, but did they leave behind an entire family? No. Did they leave behind a set of parents that now treats them like guests? No. They got wives who changed themselves to fit into their new families—and for what? Can they genuinely say they give their wives all the happiness they deserve for making all the sacrifices they made? Can they genuinely say that the cattiness of the mother-in-law is worth the love they got from their husbands? Can they say their offspring make it worth the amount of work they've put into their lives?

I scan the room and find Kabir chatting to Jack. He catches my eye and we smile. There's warmth in that brief look.

Would Kabir make my sacrifices worth it? I know I shouldn't be thinking about Kabir that way, and I am not, not really, but I can't help but wonder. Had he been in Dubai for the long term, had we met in different circumstances, could this have been something other than the serious-casual dichotomy we're juggling?

As I turn back to face the couple, my phone vibrates.

Kabir: You look gorgeous today x

I smile and look up. My mother is staring at me with a disappointed look. I can almost hear her saying 'Can you get off your phone for a bit, please? Your best friend is getting married.'

Having my mother here is turning out to be slightly inconvenient. She, along with all the other parents and family friends only joined the celebration yesterday, but it means Kabir and I can't be that open about our goings-on. Although we haven't expressly stated to anyone that we've been managing a 'side hustle' all this while, everybody has worked out that a pull situation has occurred and that we've decided to see it through until the end of the wedding.

Carrying that out whilst my parents hovered, though, is slightly weird, so we haven't been in the same room alone together in a whole day. For a relationship with carnal roots, this is not working out so well for us.

Alia: You don't look too bad yourself
Kabir: I leave tomorrow

I feel a drowning sensation in my stomach. Of course. We are at the wedding. This was bound to happen. Everyone is checking out tomorrow. This solemn wedding venue is a reminder that all the parties are over and reality is kicking in. For Meher and Akash, and for everyone else in the room who is currently experiencing any semblance of a hangover. The biggest hangover is yet to come: going back to normal life.

I want to tell him I don't want him to go. I want to tell him I'll miss him. But there's no point. Yes, of course, I'll think about him for a long time. But does that change anything? No. The reality stays the same. Just because desire exists, reality cannot be altered.

Kabir: Will I see you tonight?
Alia: Definitely

The wedding ends and everybody gathers for lunch. I feel like the protagonist of a Bollywood film where the actress is lonely at a party and keeps looking at her love interest while sad music plays in the background because they both know that a union between the two is not possible. So, we pose for photos with the couple, we dance back at the hotel, and we join in the general banter. I don't know if he feels the way I do or not, and I would rather not know.

At the end of the evening, Kabir drops me a text to say that he will see me in five minutes in my room. He brings shawarmas and fizzy drinks, something I had gone on about as the best drunk food to ever exist. I'm touched that he remembers. Is this what it feels like when you're with someone you have genuine feelings for? I hug him tight when he has to leave, wanting to soak up the warmth in his skin. He caresses my skin lightly in silence. I think back to when we first met, the whiff of smoke he was seemingly bothered by.

I could do with another smoke.

Paradigm Shift

Returning to work after a holiday is like being woken up in the middle of the night by a fire alarm. The anxiety is exactly the same. You stumble around looking for your phone, keys, and shoes to get out of the house, much like you check your inbox after a holiday, trying to find that one email you would like to start your return-to-work journey with. When everything is well and you find out the alarm was just a drill, the sense of calm returns, much like when you clear your inbox and realise that normality can resume.

For the first few days after returning to work, I pretty much stumbled around, trying to navigate my 250 unread emails. About fifty were promo emails. There were meetings I had to attend, which invariably started with 'How was the wedding, Alia?' or 'Mate, that was a lot of outfit changes', or my least favourite, 'When's yours?' I have one mother in Abu Dhabi asking me that question; I don't need another one asking me that in Dubai. My favourite question comes from Aisling: 'Can I do a dance recital for your wedding? Whenever it happens.'

I am determined to work as late as I have to, to get through my pending tasks from the previous week. It will keep me distracted from thoughts of Kabir. Luckily, he isn't very active on social media and is more of a story viewer than a story creator.

His face doesn't usually pop up on my social media, although it's a different story when friends tag us both in posts with '#takemeback' sprawled across the caption. Then his face does pop up and I sigh like a lovelorn actress in a war film.

Still, it isn't as bad as it could have been. We had an amicable goodbye and an even more amicable tenure together. There was no irrational yelling or breaking of anyone's trust. The slate was at its cleanest.

But it is this very quality of the Kabir situation that bothers me. The slate was clean. Feelings hadn't changed for anyone and no breaking of trust had happened. And yet, there was a finish line. It was as if the Universe wanted to play mean pranks on me. For years, Mum and Dad badgered me about getting on the marriage/rishta wagon and when I finally felt ready for something meaningful—not marriage, just something meaningful—he too turned out to be flighty, and through no fault of his own.

I'm not entirely heartbroken, no. Kabir and I hardly know each other. Just over a week hardly qualifies as a relationship.

I'm not disappointed either. I knew exactly what I was getting into and for how long. The finish line was clearly drawn from the off and nobody owed anyone anything.

I am angry though. I'm angry that I can't channel any anger toward a person or a situation. I can't be upset because I haven't been wronged. Perhaps if Kabir hadn't been so perfect, I might have been able to bury my feelings deep inside. Years later, I would have uncovered those feelings and they would have been part of a happy memory. *Oh, yes, Kabir,* I would think. *He was lovely.* Now those feelings are part of a memory that starts with *what if,* and I hate that.

But feelings are just like nail varnish remover. If left open and unattended for too long, they evaporate. Thus, not too long later, I find myself in a pleasant mood again. Whether it is because all feelings are gone or because I have completed all my tasks at work is anyone's guess.

Life is somewhat sane again. Well, as sane as it ever is. I'm back at the gym in an effort to pump out the wedding-week alcohol from my body, and I now sleep at human hours again instead of Indian wedding hours.

As a side effect of the wedding, though, Mum and Dad have renewed talks of my pending nuptials with a TBC groom and reactivated my account on IndianRishtaa.com. I can't say I'm surprised. I had a feeling this would happen, but I didn't realise it would happen so soon after Kabir.

When Mum sends me profile IDs of eligible men, I think about Kabir. Kabir exists. Surely, if one Kabir exists, there has to be someone else like him. The world can't have just the one Kabir and then a group of idiots from IndianRishtaa.com. It just can't be how the world functions. And if there is a second Kabir somewhere, shouldn't I wait for him, or look for him, before giving in to one of these IndianRishtaas?

And where will we find this new Kabir? ...Clink? Sassy Alia rolls her eyes and takes another swig of ouzo.

Since coming back from Abu Dhabi, I'm starting to view Clink more favourably. Perhaps it isn't Clink's fault that my online dating experience has been, for lack of a better word, shite. Perhaps it's me. Do I know my purpose of being on the platform? Do I know what I'm looking for in a man? Am I sticking to these standards? Probably not, because these are things I haven't given a second—or even first—thought to since joining Clink.

I reactivate my account. Clink might not be so bad. I have a better idea of what I want. I want someone nice. I don't want someone mucking me about anymore. I don't want to be ghosted. I don't want to be stood up. If there is a connection, I want to harness it instead of giving up just because neither the guy nor I want to text first. Surely, these are childish habits and I am not a child anymore. Is this what growing up feels like? Should I phone Mum and Dad and tell them that they are one step closer to having the model daughter they've always wanted me to be?

'Alia, you should take this seriously', Mum always says to me. Guess what, Mum? It's happening. I'm taking this seriously.

After a few minutes on Clink, though, I find nobody to swipe right on and decide against telling my mother about any such paradigm shift. It appears that I am ready, but the Universe is not.

Maybe this was the point of Kabir. Maybe Kabir was a gift from the Universe, for me to experience a no-pressure escapade for a week, as short term as it gets, and see for myself something I've yet to experience. Maybe he was meant to be a benchmark. Maybe the Universe thought, *Next time you find someone, Alia, make sure he tells you regularly how beautiful you are and calls you and texts you and makes you feel special. Anything less than that is second best and it's as Madonna says: don't go for second best, baby.*

So here I am, a twenty-five-year-old Indian Millennial, getting life advice from Madonna.

Double Date

I miss having a female best friend to vent to about being made to chat to IndianRishtaa sample pieces. Sanjay is lovely but he is a man, and sometimes he offers life advice instead of just an ear. I don't need a solution. Stop telling me how I should deal with my parents. Stop telling me it's my life. Stop telling me my parents can't control my life. You don't think I know this? You don't think I know my own parents? You don't think I have tried every single route out of this? Believe me when I say there is no way out. The only way out is to get sucked deep into the black hole, deep enough that I emerge from the other end as a woman married to one of these samples, and I have more steel in me than that to give up and give in already.

But I hit up Sanjay anyway while Meher and Akash are on their honeymoon in the Maldives. When we get to the bar, we spend the first half an hour scrolling through Meher's social feed and stories, fuming with jealousy at the private hut and access to the ocean that she and Akash are so obviously enjoying.

'Well, it's not so bad here, I suppose', I say, looking around at the bar we've chosen for today. It's a quaint little pub, in fact, with a massive Christmas tree to the side and the football playing on the telly.

Sanjay shrugs. 'I could have been out on a date', he says simply.

'Hey, no one asked you to come!'

'I'm joking!' he says. Then, 'Are you in the mood for some bad decisions?'

'How do you mean?'

'Get on the pull a little bit.'

'There's literally nobody here', I say, looking around again, inwardly retracting my statement about it not being so bad. This Friday night we have somehow managed to choose the most boring pub on the planet.

'I think it might be time to set you up on a date with someone I know', Sanjay says with a grin. 'Obviously you'll have to set me up with someone too.'

'What? You've found someone, then?!'

'Yes', Sanjay nods with a broad smile.

'Who?!'

'Newly appointed junior partner in my company. He's literally a baller, and he's only thirty!'

I stare at him for a second. Clink is getting me nowhere. IndianRishtaa is getting me closer to wanting to kill someone every day. Could this be worse than that? Probably not. Probably worth a try. Nothing to lose, right?

'Photo', I order.

Sanjay pulls out his phone and shows me Neil's social media photos. *Neil Shergill.* He seems rather attractive. He looks tall and lean in his pictures, his black hair gelled back so he looks quite proper and professional, and a light stubble on his face. There are photos of him in traditional Indian attire from what looks like Indian weddings. His name screams Punjabi and already I feel a level of familiarity with him. There is one photo with a man who looks like him, maybe his brother, and another photo with a little girl, making funny faces at the camera. Again, I assume it's a niece or a cousin. If he is trying to manipulate women into thinking he is lovely with children, it's working.

'Cute enough', I say with a nod, giving him his phone back.

'Cute enough?' Sanjay says. 'He's gorgeous!'

'Do you want to go out with him instead?'

'Trust me, if I was gay, I'd ask him out.'

'So, now you want me to find you someone?' I say.

'Yes, please', he says with a wide smile.

'Literally, all my friends are either dating or engaged', I say, mentally ticking my list of friends. *Selina: engaged, Ashleigh: engaged, Lalita: engaged for the past two years, Anisha: recently engaged, everyone else: not been in touch for the longest time.*

'What about friends of friends? Surely, there must be someone!' Sanjay insists.

I sigh. I did have my eyes on someone for Sanjay a long time ago but setting them up had been a challenge. I met Priti through a friend, and she seemed cool, but getting her and Sanjay's availability to match had somehow not worked. Perhaps all the planning made it clinical. Maybe this is what we need, a little spontaneity.

'Okay, I might have someone for you', I say, pulling my phone out to show him Priti's photo.

Sanjay nods. 'Oh, yeah, she's pretty.'

I dial Priti's number.

'Wow, we're phoning each other now?' she says when she answers the phone.

I chuckle. 'Yes, this is a phoning material conversation. What are you up to right now?'

'Can you believe it, for the first time in ages I'm home on a Friday night. I'm having a chill one.'

I look at Sanjay with a grin.

'Okay, get dressed, we're going out.'

'What?' Priti is clearly confused. I explain that I have a guy for her. She groans. She asks me if he's worth getting out of bed and wearing a bra for. I assure her that he is 100 percent the kind of guy you would not regret getting dressed up for. I can sense her rolling her eyes. She agrees to meet us at Barasti in the Marina in an hour.

'Well, my job is done', I say, hanging up. 'Is Neil coming?'

'You know he is', he says with a grin.

'Wow', I say, now smiling. A double date. What makes a date daunting is going out to meet a stranger who could easily turn out to be a dickhead. But Sanjay and I have eliminated that possibility. I know Priti is cool and Sanjay knows Neil is a baller. All that's left is to match our compatibility. Now, if the Universe were to take some time off from screwing over my brain, maybe that could happen too.

Red Flags

For someone who regularly shames Barasti for being the chav-viest beach bar known to mankind, I do frequent it more than I like to admit. Sanjay and I have snagged a few sunbeds on the beach. We have a bucket of beers and we're just tipsy enough to exude a boost of confidence.

Neil and Priti arrive almost at the same time. Priti has donned a black top and black jeans, and with her black curly hair is exuding a tiger-esque aura. She is quite petite so her big hair stands out. When Neil walks in, Nether Alia reacts rather excitedly to his beige shorts and blue linen shirt. It's not exactly the warmest evening so his choice of outfit is surprising, but he looks every bit the baller Sanjay described him as. Maybe it's because I know he's a young partner in a law firm and hence a professional baller, or maybe it's his nonchalance as he walks toward us with a careless smile, but something seems to be working.

'Hi', he says, extending his hand toward me. 'I'm Neil.' He has the thickest North American accent and the huskiest voice.

'I'm Alia, nice to meet you.'

'That's a beautiful name, Alia', he says with a nod and sits down beside me on my sunbed.

A quick round of introductions later, Sanjay, Neil, Priti, and I are having a fun conversation. It's so much better to have this group effect instead of a couple effect where the focus cannot move from each other.

I learn that Neil hails from Canada, his parents having migrated from Punjab to Brampton, Ontario soon after getting married. I wonder what Mum and Dad would think of me meeting a Canadian Punjabi. Surely they'd be delighted. I've been accused of being too disconnected from my roots, and nothing gets closer to my Punjabi roots than Canada.

He tells me about his job as a lawyer and how most of his life has been about reading paperwork since the first year of university. He went to Birmingham. I think back to the number of Canadians I met at university in the UK and how they were all from Brampton as well. I teased them by asking if Brampton was the Southall of Canada. They turned rather cold before telling me that Brampton was nothing like Southall. I established that Canadians may not have the best sense of humour.

'When was the last time you were in Canada?' I ask him.

'Three years ago.'

'Oh, it's been a while then! Don't you miss your family?'

'My parents have visited Dubai since then, but honestly... since my divorce, I don't think I want to go back to Toronto.'

I look at him, taking care to keep my expression neutral. Sanjay forgot to mention this little detail. Neil's baller nature clearly outweighed his divorce in Sanjay's eyes.

'You didn't know that about me', Neil says with a smile, sipping his beer. Tipsy Alia finds this image quite sexy, a nonchalant Neil with his husky voice, but Sassy Alia seems to be looking out for me and is holding Tipsy Alia back from leaning toward Neil, exuding flirtation.

'I didn't, I say. 'You've been divorced for three years? How young were you when you got married?' I add, my thoughts pouring out with no filter.

Neil chuckles. 'Very young. I was twenty-six when I married Lily. Things didn't work out. We got divorced. It was nasty and I left Canada. Fresh start.'

'Right', I nod. 'Well, that's fair.'

'Have you had a disastrous relationship like that?'

I chuckle. 'No, I've had very short-term… experiences. Nothing disastrous yet, and nothing remotely long term.'

'How is that possible?'

I turn to look at him. 'I don't know.' I shrug. 'I've only ever met dickheads.'

'So you don't settle, then?'

'I don't need to. I have faith that there exists at least one non-dickhead in the world that I might be able to get my hands on.'

Neil chuckles. 'You're funny', he says softly.

Oh, God, this again? I'm really not in the mood to have to big up some guy and then lose my shit over him.

'I know.' I nod. 'You're alright too', I add with a grin.

'You wanna take a walk?' he says.

I agree and we walk to the bar to get another drink and then head out by the sea. Sanjay and Priti have taken their date to the dance floor. Now that Sanjay and I seem to have hit it off with our respective dates, apparently we don't need each other anymore. I don't know how I feel about Neil. He is gorgeous, there's no doubt about that. In a very basic bitch turn of events, I find his Canadian accent quite sexy too. He's a junior partner in a law firm, so he is not wanting for brains. But he is a divorced

233

man. Sure, a divorced man is not a bad man, but is he a man ready to engage in serious shenanigans, or is he still in a casual mindset? Well, no point panicking about it yet; this is but our first encounter.

As we walk along the beach, we chat about our families. He tells me he has a younger brother, who I guess is the one featured on one of his photos. He has several aunts and uncles here in Dubai, as a result of which he never truly feels like he is away from home. Eventually, he circles back to his divorce. He met Lily in a bookstore. I find this funny because I'd hoped to meet my beau somewhere more organic than Clink, like at a bookstore. Lily and Neil were in the store to buy the sequel of a fantasy novel they were both fans of. They chatted for quite some time, after which he added her on Facebook and asked her out the same evening.

Months later, Lily's family got anxious about her dating someone and staying out late until well after decent hours. Neil buckled under pressure and proposed to her. Not having known each other for more than six months, their lives turned sour after the wedding. Within the year they were divorced.

Listening to Neil's story scares me a little bit. There was love between them, he says. Lots of love. But perhaps not enough. Maybe they were too young, he says. Maybe he should have been stronger and not buckled under pressure. Maybe he should have insisted that getting to know each other was definitely more important than saving face in front of the Brampton society that was judging Neil and Lily for dating out of wedlock.

It makes me wonder, though. How does one know that they know their partner well enough to marry them? If I marry someone, how do I know it's not going to end in divorce? I barely know if a third date is forthcoming, so how would I know what the future would hold?

He tells me about all his past relationships and how he learned something new from all of them. From his high school girlfriend, he learnt not to trust someone easily or they will cheat on you. From his university girlfriend he learnt that emotional abuse is not just something you read about in the news. From his wife he learnt that a great connection isn't the only thing that makes a marriage work. Overall, he seems like quite the broken person, the prime example of Relationship Red Flags. Sassy Alia feels like a second date will not be forthcoming.

But chatting with him is fun and easy. He is witty and definitely clever. I like that he is sarcastic. I like that he is knowledgeable. We have a fair bit of banter going but we also talk about intelligent things. We talk about global politics. We talk about the economy. He finds my research job to be interesting. He has in fact watched the Dubai Opera production of *Othello*, and enjoyed it. He seems like a lovely man. Intelligent and handsome, but riddled with red flags.

A few minutes later my phone rings.

'Yes, Sanj?'

'I'm dropping Priti off at her place.'

'Oh, you're leaving? How come?'

A pause. Then he whispers, 'We're taking this back to her place.'

'Ah', I say. Well, at least one of us has had a no red flag date.

I hang up the phone and look at Neil.

'It would appear Sanjay and Priti have really hit it off and are heading out.'

'Oh, good for them.' He smiles. 'Would you like another drink?'

Ordinarily, I would. He seems nice and he thinks I'm funny. He's even told me I'm gorgeous, which is what Madonna and I agreed I'd be looking for in a man, someone who appreciates me. But the red flags and Sassy Alia keep glaring at me.

A counter-suggestion comes through from Tipsy Alia: *Well, we're here anyway, so what's the worst that could happen? You can't possibly get your heart broken after the first date.*

So we walk back into the bar, but just as we do, another phone call comes through, this time to Neil.

'Sanj?' Neil says, surprised. Then, 'Are you kidding me?'

I raise my eyebrows. Is Sanjay about to cockblock his friend and himself on the same night?

Neil ends the call with a frown.

'I am so sorry', he says, 'but apparently something is going wrong in the Chicago office and we need to get on a call with them.'

'Right now?'

'Yes, unfortunately.'

'Oh, okay', I say, low-key relieved that I can just go home instead of chatting to a good-looking man with a million red flags.

'I'm really sorry. I honestly don't want to leave', he says, taking my hand. Then he plants a kiss on my mouth, one hand holding my hand and the other hand on my waist. 'I'll see you later', he says a few seconds later.

I freeze as I watch him walk away. He turns back to look at me and waves.

No, don't do this. Do what? *You suddenly like him, don't you?* ...Yes, I'm sorry, but he had aftershave on! How can I not like him? *Fucking hell.*

I message Priti, who tells me she's pissed off that Sanjay has left her hanging. I reassure her that he would never leave like that unless it was supremely important. I get another drink and sit down with a sigh.

No. We can't lose it over him. Too many red flags. Good kisser, but too many red flags. *Good plan.*

Tragedy Averted

I usually spend the morning after a date in a state of confusion. There's some level of joy on occasion, when the man is clever and handsome at the same time and chemistry seems to be on point between us. But there's confusion all the same because I never know if things are going to move forward. This morning, however, I am more confused than ever before.

This man that Sanjay has brought into my life, this Neil... fucking hell.

I spent all of last night convinced that going out with a man displaying too many red flags is a sure-fire way of setting myself up for a disastrous relationship, something that Neil seems to have had more than his fair share of. One kiss later, though, everything has changed.

Was it just the kiss? Was it really just the kiss? Am I that easily swayed? My behaviour seems to be indicating that I am. Maybe it wasn't the kiss itself but how easy it was being with him. We did have banter and we did have intelligent conversation. Can we not just ignore the red flags?

Or maybe we just calm down because despite kissing us, he didn't actually get our number. He works with Sanj, Sassy. If he wants to get in touch, he has a way of doing it. Or social media. Or something! *I thought you said you weren't going to lose it over this man.* Yeah, well, I say shit like that all the time.

It's nearly afternoon when Priti texts me to say that Sanjay has asked her out for a second date that evening and that she's looking forward to it, thanks to me.

Great. Everybody gets a second date but me. Fab.

But I do feel a sense of relief. Had Neil asked me out a second time, I would have said yes. Maybe I'm just a sucker for a handsome, intelligent man. Maybe I'm silly enough to ignore red flags. But aren't we all? Surely, I'm not alone? Should I not be making mistakes and living my life? So, really, Neil has done me a favour by not asking me out.

I spend the rest of the day in gratitude. Maybe the lessons from Kabir were good enough to last me a lifetime. Maybe he taught me the biggest and most important lesson there is: Don't settle for second best. With Neil, I might have done that. I might have even done what Neil did with Lily. Buckle under pressure. Except Neil buckled under familial pressure, whereas I would be buckling under the pressure of my own stupidity.

So I clean the house, I do my laundry, and I cook. I engage in thoroughly non-hip and non-happening activities before sitting down to watch a film with a large bowl of curry and a bottle of wine to keep me company.

Just as I turn the telly on, though, my phone rings. It's an unknown number. If it's someone trying to sell me something at nine o'clock on a Saturday night, I am going to be pissed.

'Hello?'

'Hey, gorgeous. It's Neil.'

LOL wut.

239

'Oh! Hi, Neil', I say, setting down my bowl of curry on the table and sitting back on the sofa. Speaking on the phone! That's new.

'What's going on?' he says with his lazy North American drawl. So sexy.

'Uh... I was just about to watch a film, actually.'

'Oh, what are you watching?'

I pause. Then, '*Austin Powers*', I say, almost embarrassed. I spoke to this man last night about the opera and French cinema and today I am about to watch *Austin Powers*.

Neil laughs. 'Great movie.'

'What are you up to? How was the office last night?'

'It was... yeah, not great. But it's cool, it's done now. So listen', he continues, 'I don't know if you'd rather Austin Powers kept you company, but I'm driving around Downtown, if you would like to join me?'

I pause. I like Neil. I really like Neil. Well, not *really*, but he might be better company than Austin Powers. And yes, there are red flags, but I don't have to wave them. They can just sit there while I have my fun and then we can come up with some sort of exit route when the time comes. I don't necessarily have to deal with the flags, do I?

'How'd you know I live in Downtown?' I say finally.

Neil chuckles. 'I'm not a creep, I swear. Sanjay told me.'

'So you didn't just happen to be driving around Downtown, then?'

'No, ma'am', he says. I can hear a chuckle.

I send him my location and change my outfit quickly, glad that I didn't eat any food. If Neil is going to kiss me again tonight, I would rather not smell like curry. Within ten minutes, he drives up to the entrance of my building. Nether Alia perks up when she sees that he drives a BMW. I ask her to calm down but she has a mind of her own.

I get into the car and take a quick look around: black leather, sleek, and new. There is a mellow RnB tune playing, which makes the ambience very sexy indeed.

'Hey, gorgeous', he says and kisses me.

He's very open, Alia. Is this an American thing, or a Neil thing?

'Hi', I say with a wide smile. 'Nice car.'

'Thanks', he says, taking my hand.

What the fuck. Did he ask us before taking our hand? Where's the consent? You know, I'm starting to realise that handholding was a big thing only in our heads, not for the rest of the world.

'Your hand is cold', he says.

'I'm always cold', I say, trying to sound less nervous than I feel.

'Well', he says with a grin, 'I can warm you up.'

He asks me about my day and I tell him about the cleaning and cooking, immediately regretting telling him the less than attractive details about my life. He tells me he spoke to his family on the phone and got shit from them about not thinking about getting married. I smile at this. He asks me if I've eaten, and I tell him no. He says he knows a cafe in Downtown Dubai that serves the best shawarma.

'No offence, but I grew up in the UAE and I know for sure that that is not the best shawarma', I say. 'But, sure, we can go there.'

Neil turns to look at me. 'Where is the best shawarma in Dubai?'

'It's a little cafe in Old Dubai. You wouldn't know it, you're a Canadian, Marina boy.'

'Okay, take me there.'

'Can I drive?'

'No.'

We navigate through the streets of Old Dubai and end up in the crowded area just outside the cafe that I know serves the best shawarma in the world. The cafe is always crowded, and never in the past twenty-plus years have I known there to be a parking space available near it. So Neil double parks and I rush in to pick up the food. I also get a pack of gum because a shawarma is nothing without garlic, and I'm not about to let garlic breath get in our way.

We drive around the city while Neil discovers that he's been living under a rock. He also discovers the joys of the best shawarma in the world.

'That's all new stuff', I say, waving a hand at our surroundings as we cruise toward the highway, heading out for a long drive. 'This is authentic Dubai.'

'You grew up in Abu Dhabi though, didn't you?'

'Same same.' I shrug. 'I came to Dubai loads, of course.'

'Would you move back to Abu Dhabi?'

'Oh, fuck no. I love Abu Dhabi and I love my family, but I can't go back to living under the shadow of my parents.'

'How do you mean?'

'Well.' I sigh. 'I think we need a certain amount of distance between us so they don't get full control over my life.'

'You don't come across as someone who can be controlled by anyone.'

I chuckle. 'I try really hard not to be, but they get in my head. Anything that can get in my head is already exercising control over me.'

'Fair enough. What do they get in your head about?'

'What do you think? Twenty-six-year-old single girl, living on her own in Dubai. What could they be trying to get in my head about?'

'Ah. Marriage?'

'Yep. They won't quit until I meet "the one".'

Neil chuckles. 'Just tell them "the one" doesn't exist and move on.'

'You don't think it exists?' I say.

'Do you?'

'I don't know. I never thought about it. You clearly don't.'

'Well, let's just say, I thought Lily was the one. And we know how that ended.'

'Maybe you just made a mistake. Maybe your one is just around the corner.'

Neil chuckles. 'Yeah, I don't think so.'

Then why are we in this car? We could have had shawarma delivered.

'Oh God', he says. 'I just realised how that sounded.'

I laugh.

'I haven't been on a date in a long time, so I feel like I don't know what to say', he continues, clearly embarrassed.

'That's fine.' I smile at him. 'Although driving to Old Dubai for a shawarma doesn't really count as a date. Next time, do better.'

'You want a next time, then?' he says, squeezing my hand.

I turn to look at his face. He's grinning but he's focused on the road.

'Yes', I finally say. Sassy Alia starts protesting but I seem to have reached a point of no return.

'Good', he says and kisses my hand. Nether Alia gives me another jolt of joy.

Soon, we're back in Downtown Dubai and I surprise myself by asking Neil a question I've never asked anyone before.

'Would you like to come up for a drink?'

Neil smiles. Then, 'Maybe next time.'

Did someone just turn down our blatant offer for shenanigans? That's fucking tragic.

'Only because I have an early start tomorrow', he adds.

'Yeah, of course!'

Yeah, just pretend we aren't ridiculously embarrassed.

I walk upstairs, groaning. Why did I have to do that? This *is* fucking tragic; Sassy Alia is right.

And then my phone buzzes.

Neil: What's your apartment number?

I stare at the text. Then...

Alia: 602
Neil: Coming up

So Where is this Going?

The past month has gone by in a blur. Well, for me, mainly. For my parents, not so much. They continue to scour the internet to find me a husband.

After the unexpected events of shawarma night, I have been feeling positively drugged. It's a feeling I didn't think was possible after Kabir, but apparently it is. I knew Kabir wasn't the end of the world. And now I have been proven right.

Neil is lovely. He doesn't text. He phones. And he phones me every day after work. *Hey, Alia, wanna go for a drive? Hey, Alia, coffee? Hey, Alia, miss your face, wanna come to my place?* Alia, this; Alia, that. Alia is delighted and because of Neil's sincerity, Alia is starting to develop feelings for Neil.

I would tell my parents about Neil so they could relax a little bit too, but I can imagine how that conversation would go. I would tell them I'm seeing someone as more than a friend, and they would ask to meet him. If I propose this to Neil, he will run, thanks to his divorce trauma. I do confide in Trisha, and she agrees with me. She also asks me why I've decided to date the man with the highest number of red flags in the history of relationships, to which I have no answer.

I am not fazed by this, though. I see Neil often enough to know that despite the red flags, his interest in me is consistent.

'Yeah, you've been seeing him loads, haven't you?' Sanjay says to me one evening.

'Yes', I say with a grin.

'Just be careful', he says.

My expression drops from satisfied grin to unexpectedly slapped in the face. 'What do you mean?'

'Well, he's had a rough time. He went through a lot of shit. You know he's divorced, right?'

'Yeah, that's a piece of info I should have got from you before we went out, not from him during our date', I say, pursing my lips.

'Yeah, sorry', Sanjay says with a shrug. 'But I didn't think you'd get serious about him.'

'Why did you not think that? What was the purpose of setting us up? Aren't you and Priti still seeing each other?'

'Well, yes, but... I just thought you could do with a night out. I didn't think you'd date him. I thought you'd realise he's a broken man.'

'Are you fucking joking?!'

'Look, he's a top lad, honestly, but just be careful. Maybe I'm wrong. Maybe he's over his shit and really likes you too.'

'Well, how am I meant to find out?'

'You could talk to him. As a guy, I can tell you, that's not our favourite thing to do, but it might be your only option.'

'Well, as Alia, I can tell you, it's not my favourite thing to do either! Fucking hell, Sanj! It's *my* job to find me emotionally unavailable men, not yours.'

Sanjay's words bother me, but only until I get another call from Neil. And then another. He speaks to me at the end of the workday and before he goes to bed, and nothing about him makes it seem like he's a broken man. Sassy Alia continues to protest, but I don't see anything wrong with him, so I don't believe there's anything wrong with him.

It's also the longest I have ever been involved with a man. A month. That's a milestone for me. I'm not going to celebrate it like an attention-hungry couple on social media, but I refuse to not be happy about it.

Come the weekend, Neil phones me to ask if I would like to do a little day trip up to the mountains just outside of Sharjah, bordering Oman. We set out at midday. It's a beautiful afternoon. Just breezy enough that the glaring sun doesn't become unbearable, and hardly humid. We stop at a local farm for fresh fruit. We crank up our favourite tunes. We climb up the mountain and sit by the freshwater stream. When the sun sets, it is unbelievably romantic and the only thing stopping us from canoodling is the police car parked in front of us.

How could I possibly believe this is a broken man? In my experience, fuckboys don't usually make the effort to take girls up to the mountains. The only climbing they are usually willing to do is in and out of beds and preferably their own.

We drive to town, slightly tired but feeling a bit closer than before. It's the longest time we've ever spent together and we haven't bored each other. Maybe this is a sign that things are only going to get better? We arrive in Downtown around ten o'clock, exhausted. We've spent the last half an hour in comfortable silence, but then Neil's phone goes wild with notifications.

'Ugh', he groans. 'Clink keeps sending me notifications even though I haven't looked at it in like a month.'

'What do you need it for? Just delete it', I say, rubbing my eyes. So far, Clink has been utterly useless, so really, why anybody still continues to use it is a mystery to me.

'Is that what you want me to do?' Neil says slowly.

I look up at him and realise how he may have heard that. Girl he's been dating for a month asks him to delete a dating app. It kind of sounds like a where-is-this-headed conversation is coming.

Well, fuck my life.

'I didn't— I didn't mean it that way, I just mean that it's an annoying app.'

'It is.' He nods and sets his phone down. 'But do you think maybe we should have a chat about us?'

Seriously. Fuck my life. You're trying so hard, just do it.

'Sure', I say. 'We're in a locked car on the highway, no way for me to escape.' I laugh nervously.

'I like you', he starts. 'I really like you. I haven't laughed as much as I do when I'm with you in a long time.'

'But?'

Neil laughs. 'But I won't delete Clink.'

Told you he's bad news. Seriously, Alia, you should listen to me.

'I won't delete Clink because we aren't in a committed relationship. I'm not seeing other women, but we aren't committed either.'

I pause. Then I nod. 'That's fair.'

'How about you, where are you at?' he asks.

Okay, he's making us talk about our feelings, why do you even like this guy?

'I'm... happy with what we have going. I'd like to just go with the flow and see where this goes.'

Neil nods and signals for me to continue.

'I'm not in a rush for anything to materialise with us', I say.

I'd love to hear you say that in front of Mum and Dad.

'Good.' Neil nods and takes my hand again.

When he drops me home I think about the conversation. Had I been 100 percent honest? I think so. I do want to go with the flow and see where things go instead of rushing to an outcome. What good could rushing do? Why not just let things run their course? Am I doing what Madonna said I should do? I don't think Neil is acting like a second-best character in any way. Sure, he isn't deleting Clink, but he isn't treating me like a second-best presence in his life either. We've just had a magical day up in the mountains before I ruined it by speaking without a filter. Until that moment, I didn't feel second best at all.

You're feeling it a little bit now, though, aren't you? Not entirely. If anything, he's being open and honest. I might even respect him more for this.

Sassy Alia rolls her eyes and walks away.

Three Little Words

These past few months have been enough to completely turn my world around. Mum and Dad seem to have given up on IndianRishtaa.com, to my huge relief. Work has been very satisfactory, with more research being piled onto my existing plate of work. It sounds boring, but it really is so much fun for me. I continue to work with Raj, but so much has happened since Raj that I barely think about that awkwardness.

Neil and I are closer than ever. We go shopping together, a task that Neil absolutely detests. If there's a task you absolutely hate, surely the person you ask to accompany you is someone who can make the task less awful for you? Surely, as the person making the task less awful, I have a position of significance in his mind? Surely, that means Sassy Alia can stop being angry with me, and Sanjay can stop asking me to be careful, and Trisha can stop assuming we have an end-date looming in our near future?

'Look, it's all too much to handle', Trisha insists. 'Divorced, and Canadian, and trust issues. It's just a lot of work for you.'

'Why is his being Canadian work for me?'

'Well, it's a different culture, isn't it? Forget about Canada, what about the trust issues?'

'We could workshop through them, couldn't we?'

Trisha shrugs. 'If you say so. It just seems to me that if a relationship requires this much effort so early on, it's probably not too late to exit from it. You could find someone much better, with fewer issues.'

Trisha has been married for long enough to know what makes relationships work, so I should take her advice. But I also feel like all relationships are unique, and if putting in work now would mean a future of no issues, I am willing to do that. Neil is a nice man and I like him. He's introduced me to his friends from Toronto. His inner group. They love me. They knew Lily and now they know me, and they tell Neil that I am definitely better than Lily. Apparently, I socialise with them and make the effort to get to know them. I make them laugh. I join in the banter. I'm a keeper, they say.

I tried to introduce him to my friends, too, of course. Sanjay, he already knows, but I'd be delighted if he could meet Meher and Akash too, and everyone could see for themselves how nice Neil is and that unlike what Sanjay thinks, I am not headed into a player's trap. But every time I try to make this happen, either Meher or Neil is unavailable.

The most recent attempt was foiled because Neil's car broke down mere minutes before he was meant to set out to meet us. Sanjay seems to think that 'the car breaking down' ploy is the oldest in the book for players who don't wish to get serious with their flames. I retort that Neil is a lawyer and a successful one, so if he ever wanted to find ways to get out of seeing me or my friends, he could find literally any other excuse. Sanjay scoffs at me.

Sanjay continues to scoff at me when Neil randomly disappears on me. I don't think much of it. He always reappears within a day or two. I can't expect Neil to be online 24/7, but Sanjay seems to think that no man in the history of dating has ever taken more than a few hours to reply to someone they're genuinely interested in. I decide I don't want to spend any more energy wondering why someone isn't replying. There are many more important things that one can do with their very limited time. Instead, I think about some of the nicer things Neil has done that prove he is not playing me, and that taking some time to reply to me is not the end of the world. Sanjay insists that I should question him about his behaviour. I reject the idea like a fish rejects the air upon being caught in a net.

He has introduced me to his colleagues, who think I'm hilarious. Really, if Neil ever wanted a seamless blend where his professional relationships, personal friendships, and romantic relationships fit together, he needn't look beyond me.

Meher is delighted. She thinks if Neil makes me happy, I should ignore what the haters (i.e., Sanjay) keep saying. Meher says that trust issues don't necessarily mean the end of the road, but she is also a romantic, having met her own husband through a digital fairy tale, so I'm not sure how much of her advice I want to take.

I think about a lot of things about us. I wonder when we will post a photo of us together on social media. No cheesy caption, but just a photo of us together. Doesn't even have to be on the feed; just a story will do. I wonder when we can go on holiday together, or a mini break. A weekend trip to Ras Al Khaimah, or Fujairah, or even the Palm would be perfect. I wonder why I get sad when he's sad, and jubilant when he's happy. I wonder why my mind is always occupied by thoughts of Neil. It's been nearly eight months. Surely, by now, I should think of him as a constant and start thinking about other things too.

I know why, but you won't like the answer. You know? *Yeah. It sounds to me that despite warning you, you've fallen for this man.* That's ridonkulous, Sassy, and you know it. *No, what's ridonkulous is that you know I make sense and you won't believe it.*

I think about Sassy's words. Could she be right? Could I have... fallen?

I open a new tab on my browser on the computer and type in *how quickly can you develop romantic feelings for someone?*

Several websites about being in love load as the search results. I click on the top result.

Three dates is a good rule of thumb. This isn't a hard and fast rule, but let's say you spend two to three hours together on each date, with some texting or phone time in between.

I sigh.

Then, *How long does it take to fall in love?*

Men normally fall in love within 88 days of seeing someone and women usually take about 134 days to say the three little words.

I do a little bit of maths in my head. We are well past the 133-day threshold.

Well, fuck. Fuck, so I'm in love now? What am I meant to do now? *You could tell him.* I am not telling him that we're in love! *No, not we. Only you are in love with him. I'm still mad at him for not deleting Clink.*

I sigh. Even my own insides are not supporting me.

I could ignore these feelings. I could, couldn't I? Until he says something? How healthy is that? Not super healthy, I reckon, but I was in love with David Preston for the longest time and I kept that in for more than a year. I did end up with trust issues after, but I recovered. I'm doing so well now. Getting over David was literally one of the hardest things I've ever done, so, surely, if Neil goes tits up, I could get over him too.

Terrible plan, Alia, really.

I spend the rest of the week ignoring the butterflies in my stomach every time I hear from Neil. Then one night, something happens.

'Hey, Alia.' I hear when I answer groggily. I check the time. It's two in the morning.

'Is everything okay?' I say, jolting up.

'Yeah, it's all good', Neil says. 'Sorry, I'm a bit drunk. I went out with colleagues.'

'Where are you?'

A pause. Then, 'Downstairs.'

A pause. 'Fucking hell, Neil, are you booty calling me at two in the morning?'

'No! Ugh, can I come up?'

'Yes, of course you can come up.' I groan and get out of bed to buzz him in.

When he stumbles in, I'm cranky. 'This better be good.'

'I was, um… talking to the guys', he says, sitting down on the sofa and taking the glass of water I hand him, 'and they made me realise that… I might be falling in love with you.'

I stare at him.

'I think I'm in love with you', he says again.

I blink. My heart has done multiple jolts already and I'm slowly breaking into a smile.

'Well', I start, walking toward him. 'I have to say, this is worth waking up at two in the morning for.' I sit on his lap, my arm around his shoulders.

I wonder how to say it to him. I've never said the L word to anyone apart from my family and Meher and Sanjay, and with my friends I've almost always been drunk.

I swallow. Then, 'I... feel the same way.'

Neil grins. 'That's the best you can do?'

I chuckle. 'I love you.'

Look at that. Three little words.

The next morning, Neil wakes up looking as hungover as I expected him to. He says three more words.

'Where am I?'

Here is a list of three little words that might have been better:

1. You look beautiful.
2. What a morning.
3. All day breakfast.

Although really, anything would have been better than 'where am I?' That he wasn't aware that he is in my flat is indicative of his lack of awareness of anything else that transpired, including his drunken confession of love.

'You're in my flat. Do you not remember last night?'

Neil rubs his eyes as he groans. 'Fuck', he says. 'I remember... getting to the bar. Drinking a lot. Getting a taxi. Now I'm drawing a blank.'

Sassy Alia starts laughing. *Oh, Neil, I'm in love with you. Oh, Alia, I'm in love with you. Feeling silly yet? Fucking hell. Just go and live in a cupboard under the stairs now, seriously.*

'Like, nothing?'

'Oh God, did I try to force you into doing something you didn't want to?'

I sigh and smile. 'No', I say. 'You just drunkenly stumbled in. That's all.'

I Love You...?

Every single time Sassy Alia and Sanjay conspire to make me believe that Neil might be bad news, he goes above and beyond for me. Every time someone tries to put him down, he brings himself back up. And that's why I enjoy this game between Sanj and Sassy on the one side and me and Neil on the other.

Sanjay and Sassy insist that because he doesn't remember his drunken confession of love means it's just a drunken revelation, like the time I decided to move back in with Mum and Dad and then decided against it the next morning. But the very next day, Neil apologises for being a drunken tit and offers to take me to Palm Island for a romantic getaway. Do fuckboys do that? Do casual freeloaders of sex do that? I would think not. Fuckboys and casual freeloaders only make just enough effort to land themselves shenanigans. They do the bare minimum. But that's not Neil.

'Are you justifying this to me or yourself?' Sanjay says the day before Neil and I are due to set out.

'I don't have to justify anything', I say. 'Look, it's a beautiful hotel and beautiful weather. It's going to be very romantic. I'm sure a sober confession is coming.'

I am sure of it, in all honesty. Who can escape the Romantic Gods? Even I, the least romantic person I have ever known, am prepared to be captivated by the Romantic Gods when we go for romantic walks on the beach or listen to smooth jazz at a fine dining restaurant while drinking the finest wine. The purpose of a romantic getaway is to reignite things. Why would anyone reignite things if they were looking to kill things?

Neil and I set out on our romantic getaway to the hotel I picked out for us. The room is large with a king-size bed and a bathroom as big as my room at home. The ceiling is a groovy purple with small disco balls hanging off it. If I ever wanted to host an '80s theme party, this might be the ideal venue. The balcony has a direct view of the sea, and it honestly does not get better than this. This can't be what a relationship with a red flag–riddled man looks like. Sanjay and Sassy are wrong. There is peace and sunshine and the sound of waves against the coast. This doesn't feel like it's going to have a painful end.

Come the evening, we set out to a seafood restaurant and enjoy a lovely dinner against the backdrop of the Marina sky-line with live jazz and soulful music. When we get back to the hotel, there is a strange sense of contentment in the air and a feeling of attachment to Neil that I've never experienced before. I wonder if Neil feels the same sense of contentment, the same attachment. Maybe a little? Only he can tell. But he says nothing. No sober 'I love you' tonight.

Maybe he just needs time. Maybe he wasn't really ready to say it when he did say it, and now he wants to choose the moment. After all, the last time he said the L word was to Lily. Maybe he wants to ensure that this time around it's with the right person.

The next morning we head downstairs for breakfast and then find sunbeds in the perfect spot. We wade into the pool to cool off and Neil tells me stories about his time in high school. He tells me his high school girlfriend's name was Barbara. I laugh.

'What's so funny?'

'Barbara is the whitest name I have ever heard! It's like the name of a sixty-seven-year-old white woman from... Georgia.'

'That's very specific.'

'Come on, Barbara is not a sexy name.'

'Oh, Alia is?'

'Yes, Alia is a very modern, sexy name. Did you ever think you'd have a girlfriend with such a sexy name?'

'Girlfriend?' Neil chuckles. 'That's a bit much. Don't push it.'

Say what, now? *Well, this is fucking tragic.*

Neil's phone rings and he climbs out of the pool to take the call. I feel like I have suddenly woken up from a long and elaborate dream. You know those dreams that are so good that when you wake up you're disappointed you were sleeping? I feel like I've just woken up from one of those.

I climb out as well and Neil looks at me. I signal to him that I am going to head upstairs. He gives me a thumbs up.

For the past eight months I've been feeling like I was drugged and just having the best time. Now I feel like I've gone clean and am reacting quite badly.

Did I imagine the past eight months? The drunk 'I love you' happened, didn't it? I go back to my call log. There are several calls from Neil but there's one at two in the morning from the day he said the L word. Surely, I couldn't have imagined that. I couldn't have imagined the late-night phone conversations.

I'm on a mini break with this man right now! What kind of person goes on a mini break with a casual paramour? What kind of person says 'I love you' to a casual paramour and then pretends like nothing happened?

The broken kind.

I roll my eyes. Not this again. But why not? Are Sassy and Sanj right?

I change into dry clothes and wait for Neil. As much as I hate talking about feelings and where things are headed, if ever there was a time to do it, it is now.

When Neil does walk in, he looks confused. 'Hey, babe', he starts, 'what happened?'

'That!' I say. 'Why do you call me babe?'

Neil shrugs. 'It's a term of endearment.'

'Why? I'm not your girlfriend.'

'Well... we are seeing each other. I'm confused. Do you have a problem with babe?'

'No, I don't', I say. 'I mean, yes, it's cheesy and I've always hated it, but I didn't mind when you called me it.'

'So, then what's the problem?'

'Why am I pushing it by calling myself your girlfriend? What have we been doing for the past eight months?'

Neil looks around uncomfortably and sits down on the bed. 'Alia, I thought we talked about this.'

'That was months ago', I say. 'Surely, things have changed since then.'

'I told you that I really like you and I still do. I mean... as far as I'm concerned, nothing has changed. We weren't in a committed relationship then and we aren't now.'

I pause. Then, 'Are you fucking joking?'

'I'm not.' Neil shakes his head. 'Where is this coming from?'

'It's coming from the fact that we've been seeing each other for some time now, but I'm pushing it if I put a label on us.'

Neil sighs.

I feel angry but I am still calm. I walk over to him and sit next to him on the bed.

'We're on a mini break in a romantic hotel', I say. 'Is it so crazy to think that I might be your girlfriend?'

'It is, a bit', Neil says, turning to look at me. 'I told you I didn't want to rush into anything after Lily.'

'I'm not asking you to rush into anything. You're the one who showed up at my house at two in the morning to tell me you love me.'

Neil looks at me with a frown. Then he freezes.

'Yeah.' I nod. 'That happened.'

'Look, that was a mistake', he says. 'I'm sorry, I don't... I don't *love* you.'

I feel like I've stepped on a piece of shattered glass. His words literally feel like daggers. Like stepping on a block of Lego in the dark. Like stubbing your toe against the bed. Like you've ordered a burger after a juice cleanse but the restaurant gives you a salad. This isn't what I ordered. I was expecting an 'I love you'. I got the complete opposite. I literally got an 'I don't love you'.

'You don't love me', I say. 'And I'm not your girlfriend.'

'I'm sorry, Alia.' He sighs again.

'So', I start, 'riddle me this. What are we?'

'I don't know... Friends?'

I stare at him. 'We have ridiculously hot sex for friends.'

'You know what I mean—'

'No, I think you're doing friendship wrong.'

'Come on! We're more friends than we are partners!' he snaps.

A pause. Then, 'Right.'

I stare into the distance, at nothing. I can hear Neil speaking.

'You know what I've been through with Lily', he says. 'What do you want me to do after that? Tell me, what should I do?'

I turn to stare at him. 'You should leave.'

'What?'

'You should leave. We used my loyalty points to book this room. You are not my boyfriend. So, you should leave.'

'What, you'll stay here by yourself?'

'It's my room, I can do whatever.'

'So, you're going to be petty about this?'

'No, I'm just doing what I should have done a long time ago.'

Neil gets up and starts to pack. I sit quietly and unlock my phone. No messages. No emails. Nothing I can pretend to care about while he packs. Ten minutes later, he reappears in front of me, this time with a packed suitcase.

'Is this really what you want me to do?' he says, looking at me dejectedly.

'No', I say slowly. 'But you don't want to do what I want you to do.'

The Actual End of the Road

It is ten o'clock on Sunday night and I look nothing like the powerful fierce woman I set out to become when I moved to Dubai. I am on the sofa in my shabbiest sweats, a bowl of untouched popcorn on the coffee table and a half-full bottle of wine in my hand. My other hand is scrolling through restaurants available to deliver in my area. I close the window and switch to texts. I click open Neil's window and see that he is online. A few seconds later, he goes offline. And then online again. I stick around to see if his status will change to 'typing...' but it doesn't so I switch to another tab and type in a message.

Alia: Would you like to come over? Please?

My mind is clouded with thoughts about what went wrong. The answer I get from Sassy is, well, me. I was the thing that went wrong. Yes, Neil told me he loved me. Yes, he phoned me every day. Yes, he was the perfect non-boyfriend boyfriend. But he refused to label anything. By every definition of the term, he was a fuckboy. I got played not by Neil but by my own stupidity and lack of purpose. What was I even looking for when I said yes to seeing Neil after our beach escapade? I didn't know then and I don't know now. I always knew he wasn't looking for something serious, so what was I after? I can't ask for sympathy from anyone because my current sadness is a result of my own lack of intelligence. I used to pride myself on my intelligence. I can't anymore. I'm not Neil's girlfriend, he doesn't love me, and I am not clever.

I promptly burst into quiet sobs. For the first time in my life I felt something close to love and today it's over, just like that. Nobody wronged me. Well, Neil did, a bit. If he was going to play me, he could have done it right here in Dubai; a trip to the Palm was excessive. But in the absence of his utterance of the L-word, he was always clear about his intent. Was he, though? Fuckboys traditionally ghost their gullible paramours within a few weeks, but my fuckboy religiously phoned me multiple times every day. It's as if Neil is shit at being a boyfriend but even worse at being a fuckboy.

I can't believe I live in a world where my inner sassy monologue is my only anchor. Have I been wrong about Sassy this whole time? I kept thinking she's just an internal, almost bipolar disturbance. Is Sassy my gut? Have I been shaming Sassy for the longest time for knowing what I truly want and need, when I should have been listening to her every word with as much attention as I would have given to a lesson in school?

The intercom rings and I open the door. Within minutes, Sanjay shows up at my door. I look at him morosely. He immediately walks in.

'Are you okay?'

'No', I say slowly, my voice cracking. 'I broke up with Neil.' Then I burst into tears again. How embarrassing.

'Oh, hun', he says, wrapping me in a hug. I am aware that my tears aren't really giving his shirt a good look, but as my friend, he took upon himself the task to console me and now he must bear the consequence.

'What happened?'

'Exactly what you said would happen', I say, sniffing.

'Ah.'

'It's okay, you can say I told you so.'

He chuckles. 'I'm not going to say that. Do you want to talk about it?'

'No. I want to get drunk. And then I want to cry. Do you have plans tonight?'

'No.'

'Good.'

So we open a fresh bottle of gin and watch *Bride and Prejudice*, the Indian version of *Pride and Prejudice*.

Sanjay asks me why I opted for this film.

'Neil hated it', I say.

As the movie progresses, my mind begins to wander. That was eight months of my life I won't see again. What now? What does one do after the end of a relationship? And what was the point of it?

When I entered the dating market, I was so full of hope. I was so sure I would find someone and Mum and Dad's attempts on IndianRishtaa.com would be futile and we would all be able to move on from the horrific sample pieces. But I unleashed even more horrors after. I unleashed people chicken enough to ghost people instead of telling them the truth. I found people strange enough to not even show up for dates. I met people who for no real reason will ghost you after an enjoyable second date. I met people who will tell you they love you and then forget about it. I have met people who seem perfect but live thousands of miles away.

Have they all taught me something? Maybe. Ishaan taught me that too much sweet talk must not be trusted. Puneet from Punjab taught me that a nice face does not mean a nice personality. The highly qualified Harjit taught me that educational qualifications mean nothing if you're a dick. The gorgeous Kabir taught me that I shouldn't settle for second best... And then I immediately fell for Neil, so maybe my learning style needs to be addressed.

Maybe not everything is meant to be a lesson. Maybe some experiences are just experiences. Maybe experiences are what make you who you are.

I turn to look at Sanjay. I think about Meher. I think about the three of us in school and then together at uni and then coming back to Dubai. I think about how one text prompted Sanjay to drop everything to come comfort me. Even though the only real task he has undertaken tonight is to watch *Bride and Prejudice*, he does it gracefully. I am grateful he is here. I am not yet grateful for the circumstances that brought him here, but I'm sure one day I will be grateful for those too.

I lean back and continue to watch the film. I check my phone again. No texts from Neil.

Yes, there have been lessons. Yes, I am grateful for the friends who help me through these lessons. But I am a bit pissed at Neil and a bit sad that things have ended. Will this sadness ever ease? It will. I will feel better. But better can't get here fast enough.

26

Do birthdays become more depressing every year? I feel like when I was twenty-four, I was a lot happier on my birthday than I am today, at twenty-six. To be fair, twenty-four was probably the last no-drama year I had. Twenty-five saw the creation of my IndianRishtaa.com profile. Having such a disastrous and dramatic beginning to the year should have been a warning that the rest of the year might be equally disastrous and dramatic. Now, twenty-six sees me still checking my texts to see if Neil has wished me a happy birthday. He hasn't. Because he's a dick. And I'm glad I broke up with him.

Still, it's a joyous day. The entire day has been filled with so much love. I forgot that that's what birthdays are traditionally about, not setting up accounts on Indian matrimonial websites or arguing with your parents that it's your life and you'll do whatever you please.

This birthday is delightful, but turning twenty-six has been quite tiring. I feel old and worn out. I feel like this shouldn't be happening so soon.

Still, I'm trying to look at the positives. I am in Abu Dhabi for the weekend and my parents have turned the backyard into a party gazebo that all my friends will be populating shortly. The bar is fully stocked, the music system updated, and the lights have been checked by the electrician. A bangin' party is about to occur.

Mum made my favourite breakfast and in the customary birthday morning prayer, at my insistence, she agreed to take out the bit where she would pray for a good husband for me.

'But I do want you to find a good husband, so what's wrong with praying for it?'

'Can you at least modify the prayer and say I wish Alia to be happy? Surely you want that too?'

'Fine.' And she sighed.

As the day progresses, my phone is flooded with phone calls, texts, and notifications of people sharing photos tagging me on social media. I'm not sure how I feel about my birthday being the day my friends decide to dig out all kinds of embarrassing videos of me.

When the party starts, I am in the mood for some fun. I want to forget about the year gone by. I won't be so ungrateful as to say that it was a shit year, but I do want to forget about the things that might have contributed to its occasional shittiness. So I turn to my friends and family. Trisha has arranged a dessert table with my favourite sweets, and Sanjay and Meher have put together a playlist of the hits from when we were in school. It's a cringe-worthy playlist, but we will dance to it anyway, just as we did when we were teenagers.

I think about some of the valuable lessons I have come to learn through my relatively short time on earth. I have learnt never to fall asleep with makeup on. Waking up the next morning with acne is not a good look for anyone. I have learnt a related lesson, to start thinking about skincare and not shame skincare influencers. Obviously, it doesn't have to be a complicated routine, but moisturising does not take a long time, so that's something I want to take with me into this new year.

I have learnt that it's better not to be interested in someone in a romantic capacity around your birthday because thinking about it takes up your entire day. If they don't text you on your birthday, your entire day gets ruined and, frankly, you have the rest of the year to be depressed, so leave your birthday alone.

I have also learnt that if a random past romantic interest who has previously ghosted you does wish you well on your birthday, don't think too much of it, don't reply, and definitely don't ask them follow-up questions such as how they are. You really shouldn't care.

Self-pampering on your birthday is essential. Yes, your mother did most of the work when you were born, but another year has passed in your life and you have potentially achieved nothing of significance. It's nice to pamper yourself through this realisation because your mind will produce self-deprecating thoughts on your birthday, for sure.

Your gut is queen. It took me a long time to understand that Sassy Alia isn't just a sassy monologue. She is my gut. Since realising it, we have less conflict and more agreement.

And finally, I have learnt, in the unforgettable words of Freddie Mercury and John Deacon, that 'friends will be friends'. The ones you choose to stay in touch with, anyway.

As my friends and family start pouring into the house with presents, I feel nearly festive. There will be music, dancing, drinking, good food, and celebration. And everyone is here because they care about me. These are the people I want to devote more of my time and energy to. These are the people who make me happy. Those who don't make me happy, I want to eliminate from my life. Literally Ctrl+X them out of my life. Maybe Marie Kondo and my mother have been right this whole time. Why clutter your life with people who don't bring you joy?

I have been wrong. Turning twenty-six isn't depressing. Well, it's depressing for my parents—another year older, another year single—but I am surrounded by the truest form of love I have ever known, which is the love of my family and friends. How can one be depressed when there is so much love to receive and so much love to give?

How important are Clink and IndianRishtaa.com going to be in my life? The former, probably not much. The latter, well, unfortunately it will be quite important in my parents' lives, but I don't have to let that seep into my sanity and ruin it. I can be civil to my parents about it and not argue like a teenager. Sanjay and Meher have an epiphany about how we're closer to thirty now than we are to fifteen and I chuckle.

And then it hits me. Shit. I am closer to thirty now than I am to fifteen. On this depressing note, I am going to stuff my face with cake because I am now twenty-six.

Yes, cake might be a better start than IndianRishtaa.com. Until next time.

Acknowledgements

That no man is an island is a lesson I learnt a long time ago. Massive thanks to Thalia who didn't completely lose her shit when I f***ed up massively on my final edit and handed it in two days late. Big thanks to Adele for releasing such beautiful tracks as 'Water Under the Bridge' and 'Easy on Me' that, coupled with a glass of vino, produce the most heartfelt written word. And finally thanks to Lakshmi for being a consistent reader of my work since age thirteen, from my ridiculous poetry about atoms and positrons, to how frustrated we women are.

About the Author

Amandeep was born in London and emigrated to Dubai with her family at the age of six. She is a political economist by education, fitness professional by qualification and writer by passion. She has an opinion about most things ranging from political debate across the world to Bollywood songs from the nineties and noughties that need to make a comeback. She describes her book as an account of the confused state of mind of her generation. She currently lives in Dubai with her parents and baby (her White German Shepherd).

ask_alia_

About the Publisher

The Dreamwork Collective is a print and digital publisher sharing diverse voices and powerful stories with the world. Dedicated to the advancement of humanity, we strive to create books that have a positive impact on people and on the planet. Our hope is that our books document this moment in time for future generations to enjoy and learn from, and that we play our part in ushering humanity into a new era of heightened creativity, connection, and compassion.

www.thedreamworkcollective.com
thedreamworkcollective